All He Needs For Heaven

Jim McDoniel
Chet McDoniel

Keller, Texas, USA

To order more copies, visit
www.allheneedsforheaven.com

ISBN 1441453296
EAN-13 9781441453297

Printed in the United States of America.

Preface

Since we gave birth to a limb deficient child, several people have wanted to talk to us about their suffering. Life's difficulties are so individualized that few people face a situation identical to that of another. Even if the situations look alike to observers, the relationships of the people involved and the strengths of those who are suffering make all people face suffering and sorrow as if it is peculiar to them. Yet, a commonality and kinship exists between most of us who have faced life's cruel blows, and for that reason, people have wanted to hear about Chet, our son, and how we are facing life. Upon hearing of our experience, some have indicated that they were encouraged in their own struggles. I have chosen to write to help others, and maybe, to help us.

On a few occasions, Judy and I have tried to tell an audience some of the pain and disappointment we felt at the birth of a handicapped child. While we have been willing to share our experience, we have been reluctant to share too much. We feel that the message of pain can become too painful for an audience, and that listeners can get lost in just hurting rather than hearing a message of hope. While we still speak about our feelings at the time of birth, we try not to take hearers too far into that pain, and we hope that the first chapter in this book simply informs readers of our situation. We have talked about the different subjects, that will be covered, and Judy's thoughts are interwoven with mine throughout the book.

Most people who have had a relationship with Chet feel that he has blessed their lives. He is happy and productive because of our gracious God's blessings. Chet lives his life to the glory of God. We pray that this book will help others who face difficulties live to the glory of God, also.

Contents

"SOME CONGENITAL ANOMALIES"

In 1979, Judy and I began to want another baby. We had Randy, age 9, and Jennifer, age 6, and, after much discussion and prayer, we decided to have two more children. Soon after our decision was firm, Judy's obstetrician told her that she was pregnant. Those nine months seemed to fly by. This was the happiest of the three pregnancies. Randy and Jennie were excited about having a brother or sister. Everything seemed great until the moment of birth.

When Randy was born, in 1969, I had not been privileged to be with Judy during labor or delivery. An attendant wheeled her away while I filled out papers. I was told little as I waited in that "Father's Waiting Room." At last, the doctor came out to tell me that I had a fine son. He led me to a glass window, and I saw a nurse holding a wrapped up baby. I only got to see Randy through a nursery window until the day I took both Judy and Randy home. In 1972, in Louisiana, the procedure had progressed to the point that I could be with Judy during labor, but eventually, the nurse wheeled her off to delivery while I stayed with friends in waiting room. In 1979, Judy found that Lamaze was available to us, and I readily agreed. We enjoyed the Lamaze classes and became friends with several other expectant parents in our group. I am still amazed at the principles of pain control we learned in that class. The teacher prepared us well for the big event.

From a tax standpoint, I wanted our baby to be born in December, but we waited patiently and even noticed that Judy was not as big as she had been with Randy (8lbs. 10 oz.) or Jennie (6 lbs 14 oz.). Neither the obstetrician nor we thought that Judy's size might be an indication of trouble. Finally, on January 5, Judy announced that she was having contractions.

Good friends, Micki and Elvin Campbell, came to stay with Randy, Jennie, and Judy's mother while we went happily to Bossier Medical Center to have our long awaited third child. The Campbells were to wait until the baby was born and ready to be seen, and then bring Mom, Randy, and Jenn to the hospital.

Judy's labor was exactly what the Lamaze classes had told us to expect. With the monitor in place, I could tell her exactly when a contraction was coming. She followed our coaching plan perfectly, as the pains grew closer.

A Problem Is Discovered

The obstetrician announced that the baby was breech, but that Judy would have no difficulty with that problem since this was her third child. Judy and I still had no idea of the shock we were about to receive, and the doctor did not either.

The contractions began to come too close together, and we had to hurry to the delivery room. We rolled past the obstetrician eating tamales, and Judy quickly informed him that she would not forgive him for that smell. The process of birth had turned so fast that Judy could not be given medical help, and she had Chet "naturally."

As soon as Chet's body was birthed, the obstetrician looked at me and gave a pained look. Judy's labor turned to distress.

Since Chet was breech and since he had no arms, Judy's cervix closed on Chet's neck. I blocked her view of the mirror, and called for her strongest effort in pushing the baby out. The attending nurses moved away in fear, but the skill of the obstetrician brought Chet out. Judy lay exhausted and torn badly. The doctor laid Chet on Judy's stomach and announced softly, "Now, Judy what we have here are some congenital anomalies." I leaned down next to her ear and told her plainly as much as I could about Chet's appearance. I told her that our baby boy had no arm on the right side, a short stub on the left, and short legs, as if the thigh section was missing. She had to have surgical repair immediately, but the medical personnel let us hold on to one another until the anesthetic had her totally unconscious.

Since Judy's medical condition was so urgent, Chet had been laid aside and rather left alone. When Judy was fully asleep, I walked over to Chet and began to talk to him and look him over. Soon the pediatrician came in and stitched a small cut on Chet's face. Then, he announced, "Folks, we are going to the nursery." Both doctors had shown great patience with my questions and my efforts to see and understand what they were doing. Soon the obstetrician was done, and the pediatrician came back to the doctors' lounge. There the three of us prayed.

Now to Tell the Children

While Judy was still under the anesthetic, I drove home to tell

Randy, Jennifer, Mom, and the Campbells. I have had few tasks in life that were harder. The three adults knew as soon as they saw me that something was badly wrong, but the children began to jump with joy and asked if we were ready for them to go to the hospital. I sat down on the floor and asked both of them to sit on my lap. I told them that they had a new brother, but that he came to us with some problems. After I told them about Chet's limb deficiency and that since Judy was asleep they could not go to the hospital, they were still happy and excited. Mom took them off to bed, while the Campbells held on to me.

I hurried back to the hospital, and from Judy's room, late on that Saturday evening, called all the relatives. Each phone call was difficult, but all relatives on both sides of the family pledged total support.

Judy was brought to the room just before midnight, but she was still asleep. Her doctor said that he dreaded telling her about Chet's anomalies. He was greatly relieved to hear that I had told her before she was put to sleep. She later reported that as soon as she awoke, she knew all too well that the birth and our baby's problems had not been a dream. When Judy woke up, we held on to each other and have continued to hold on to each figuratively and literally. The strength of our relationship has given us the strength to provide all Chet has needed for well being and proper development.

Sometime during the night, about two or three o'clock on

that Sunday morning, we asked the nurse to bring Chet to Judy's room. She responded hesitantly, "That is most unusual." I noted quietly that nothing about this situation was usual, and they granted our request. Judy gently undressed Chet, and we began to get acquainted with his body and soon with his personality. The nurses cared for us better than we thought possible, and we grew to love them.

Days Too Tough To Tell About

On Sunday morning, relatives and friends in distance states had a host of churches praying for us. I left Judy alone, and went to the Airline Drive Church of Christ, where I had been preaching for eight years, with Mom and the children. I had prepared a sermon which, as it turns out, would help me more than anyone who heard it that day. It was based on Deuteronomy 33:27 and entitled, "Underneath are the Everlasting Arms." After I preached, I told the church about Chet and his anomalies. A fellow minister, Wyatt Kirk, stood with his arm around me as I told them, prepared to speak for me if I could not finish the story. The church was supportive immediately, and has continued to be through the years. We will love them as long as we live for their response to our need.

I will speak little about our pain during the first months of adjusting to the cruel blow of having a handicapped child. I do not want us to have to relive those days, and I do not want any reader to loose sight of our basic message because

6

of our report of pain. We had help from friends and relatives and were able to provide everything necessary for Chet and for the rest of the family, as those necessities arose.

One day while Judy was crying and I was trying to find words of comfort and encouragement, I found one of the most important thoughts anyone can have regarding another person. I told Judy that Chet will never be able to throw a football fifty yards as the great quarterbacks can, but our other son, Randy, will never do that either. Chet does not have all he needs for this life, but he has all he needs for heaven. That thought has sustained us in several difficult hours, and it continues to be our hope for Chet. He has all he needs for heaven!

Chet Says: I have heard this story several times, but it took my reading it in a book to realize how devastating my birth was to my parents. And, yet, the irony is not lost here. While I understand the hurt and pain they felt from having to let go of a dream of a perfect child, I experienced no such devastation. I only knew happiness in my childhood, and just like most children, I had a blast growing up. When my dad and I speak together, I often comment that there was no need for them to be devastated...look how I turned out. He says my attitude and comments are exactly what they had hoped for as a product of their parenting. They did an awesome job!

2

GOD DID NOT DO IT

The theological problem of pain came sharply into focus for us at the birth of a precious boy with physical problems. We have both spoken several times to audiences since Chet's birth about God's involvement with human beings and our sufferings. Each time, we encounter people who are glad to hear that God is not the source of human suffering and that they do not have to blame God. We know that our son will face many difficulties in life, but God did not cause him to be limb deficient.

Our View of God

Several years ago, an airplane crashed in one of the eastern states, and over half of the people on board died. The plane was torn apart near the center isle. Most of those who lived were on the left side of the plane, and most of those who died who on the other side. While talking to a television reporter, one survivor declared boldly, "God was looking out for me!" What about the people on the other side of the plane? Was God not looking out for them? I am convinced that God gets blame, and sometimes credit, for what we do to ourselves as people.

Some evangelists preach a "health and wealth theology." They proclaim that if people genuinely give themselves to God, God will keep them from the difficulties of life. These evangelists teach that if you are having financial problems, all you need to do is give yourself totally to God, and all your financial problems will disappear. They teach that if you are experiencing health problems, you can be free from your pain by giving yourself totally to God. These preachers teach that relationship problems like those of a troubled marriage will quickly disappear if the people involved will just get serious about Christianity. The basic theology is that bad things do not happen to good people. People devoted to God do not have handicapped babies. Upon hearing about the birth of Chet, one former acquaintance wrote us to ask us to confess our sins and get right with God, before another bad thing happened to us.

Remember Job

Job had some friends like that one. Eliphaz, Bildad, and Zophar came to see their friend, Job, when they heard about his suffering. The fact that they sat with Job for a week and said nothing indicates that they were genuine friends. They were not trying to hurt or insult Job. They just had faulty theology, and that theology did not die with them. They took the Biblical truth that God blesses the righteous and withholds blessings from or even curses the unrighteous. But Job's friends carried that thought to such an extreme that they concluded that all suffering is the results of some particular sin. They believed that since Job was suffering, he must have done something sinful because God sends suffering to those who break his will. They kept telling Job to confess his fault, and they assured him that God would take away the suffering at that point. Job kept insisting that he had done nothing wrong. His friends believed that he had to have done something wrong, and the evidence of that wrong doing was his suffering. Throughout the book, readers today know that Job is suffering because he is good, not evil. In the end of the book, God rebuked those three friends for misrepresenting God.

In the first two chapters of Job, Satan is presented as the accuser of people and as the one who hurts people. In Job 2:3, God does accept responsibility for Job's suffering because God is the one who sets limits on Satan. However, Satan is the one who destroyed Job's possessions, killed his children, and destroyed his health. God did not do it!

Remember the Man Born Blind

In John 9, Jesus and his disciples encountered a man who had been born blind. The disciples asked a theological question, "Rabbi, who sinned, this man, or his parents, that he should be born blind?" (John 9:2, ASV) Jesus said that the blindness was not the result of a sin committed by either. There is some debate regarding verse three. I believe that he is not talking about the reason for the blindness, but is saying that it provided an occasion for the glory of God to be seen in Jesus' restoring of sight to the man. The Message translates the verse the way I believe it should be understood. Peterson represents Jesus as saying, "You're asking the wrong question. You're looking for someone to blame. There is no such cause-effect here. Look instead for what God can do." The faulty theology that was seen in Job's friends is seen in the apostles' question and again in the Pharisees' words at the end of the story. They threw the man who had been born blind out of the synagogue saying, "You were born in sin." Their evidence for saying that he had been born in sin was his blindness at birth.

Listen to James

The book of James addresses, in plain fashion, the issue of the origins of good and evil. James writes, in chapter 1:

12 Blessed is the man who perseveres under trial, because when he has stood the test, he will receive the crown of life that God has promised to those who love him.

13 When tempted, no one should say, "God is tempting me." For God cannot be tempted by evil, nor does he tempt anyone; 14but each one is tempted when, by his own evil desire, he is dragged away and enticed. 15Then, after desire has conceived, it gives birth to sin; and sin, when it is full-grown, gives birth to death.

16Don't be deceived, my dear brothers. 17Every good and perfect gift is from above, coming down from the Father of the heavenly lights, who does not change like shifting shadows.

Clearly, James is presenting a contrast of two sources. The evil comes from one direction, and the good from another. Evil comes from our own desire as we are tempted by the evil one, but good comes from God. I love the warning of verse 16 where James tells us not to be deceived about these origins. In other words, "Do not blame God for evil."

Then, There's Discipline

Hebrews 12 speaks of the discipline of the Lord. Verse 7 says, "Endure hardship as discipline; God is treating you as sons." Are we to understand that the writer is saying that God sends hardship? Was he saying that God sent the hardships those Christians were experiencing?

The book of Hebrews deals with encouraging Christians that were undergoing persecution. In chapter 11, the writer holds up several examples of people who have been persecuted and yet, held on to their faith. Chapter 12 presents these examples as a "cloud of witnesses" encouraging the Christians of that time. Then, the writer calls these Christians to consider Jesus "who for the joy that was set before him endured the cross, scorning its shame and sat down at the right hand of God. Consider him who endured such opposition from sinful men, so that you will not grow weary and lose heart." (12:2-3)

God, the Father, did not cause the cross. The opposition came from sinful men according to verse 3. God did not send the persecution that the Christians of that time were experiencing. Can you imagine a God who would put His children through the atrocities they were going through? Yet, in that same context, the writer calls for the Christians to endure hardship, and says that God was dealing with them through those hardships.

In the story of Job, Satan was clearly the one who hurt Job. Yet, God accepted the responsibility for Job's pain because He is the one who sets the limits on how much Satan can hurt us. (Job 2:3) Have you ever wondered why God did not step into history and stop the persecution of his children as soon as it started or even before it started? Wouldn't life be unreal if He did? Wouldn't people become Christians for the wrong reasons? Again, in Revelation 6, the saints who have died at the hands of persecutors ask God "How long," until He would stop the evil and punish those who were hurting His children. The answer is simply, "Not yet."

God did not send these hardships of persecution, and it is probably the same persecution in Hebrews 12 and Revelation 6. God used those horrible circumstances to the benefit of His children. God rather turned the tables on Satan who intended the persecution for evil, and God took that same horrible treatment and brought good out of it. It is unthinkable to me to suggest that God wanted His children mistreated.

Romans 8:28 promised that "all things work together for good." That passage does not say that God sends all things. It does not say that God wants us to experience all the evil comes our way. It promises that God will be with us in all of life's circumstances to make good come out of everything that comes our way.

Remember Paul

Surely the "health and wealth theologians" would not tell Paul that he needed to be more devoted to God. Paul had a "thorn in the flesh" which he asked God to remove, and God refused to remove it. In I Corinthians 12:7, Paul called that thorn, "a messenger from Satan." Notice that Paul felt that God had turned the problem into a positive benefit, but it came from Satan.

They asked "Why did God...?"

Several years ago, I was called to the hospital when good friends had lost a baby. Because of a toxic condition of the mother, the baby was born at seven months and lived only a few minutes. The young couple was in great anguish, and they still hurt today. In the middle of her crying, the young mother asked loudly, "Jim, why did God do this? Why did He take my baby? I don't understand! Why? Why? ..."

I made a mistake that day. I gave a theological answer to her cry of anguish. I explained that God did not take the baby. Her health condition was not a punishment from God, but an accident of nature, just like Chet's anomalies. The mind of that young couple was so troubled that they did not hear my theological discourse. They just hurt! I think that I should have held them tight and encouraged them to tell me about how their hearts were breaking. Perhaps many anguished cries are not intended as intelligent questions, but just hurting people trying to tell a friend that they hurt badly.

Our God is Big

Don't you think God understands when hearts are breaking?

15

He would not rush to answer a plaintive cry like that one of the young couple, and especially answer it with a deep explanation. In John 9, the disciples had a theological question when they saw the man born blind, but Jesus thought of healing him.

Psalm 46:1 announces, "God is our refuge and strength, a very present help in trouble." (KJV) God is one who helps us, not the one who hurts us! Remember Deuteronomy 33:27, "The eternal God is your refuge, and underneath are the everlasting arms."(NIV) Add Psalm 103:13 which tell of his concern for his people. The psalmist wrote, "As a father has compassion on his children, so the Lord has compassion on those who fear him; for he knows how we are formed..." (NIV)

If we cry and complain, God understands! Our God is big enough to let His children beat on His chest when they are in anguish.

No Answers

The book of Job does not answer the question of why good people suffer. When God spoke to Job, he asked a question which caused Job to say that he had spoken of that which he did not understand. Job seems to have been satisfied with his encounter with God, but God did not answer his questions. God is not going to answer our questions about Him! At least, this basic question of human suffering is not answered in the book of Job, and neither is it answered anywhere else by God.

Some experiences of suffering in the Bible do have causes named. However, none of these named causes are applicable to all situations. Job suffered because he was good. Daniel was thrown into the lion's den because he was good. However, the people of Israel suffered forty years of wilderness wanderings because of sin. Care must be taken before naming the reason for any suffering. Our greatest need in the face of human suffering is for more modesty and humility to be able to say that we do not have answers. No one scares me more that the person with clichés and quick, easy answers. We need to learn from Job's friends to come to the side of the sufferer and sit in silent, loving care, but we need to learn from those same friends to be slow to speak and slow to blame.

Chet's birth sent me back to study the Scriptures. I do not understand why God does not choose to get involved with some life situations. The renewed study has been valuable, and has reinforced my view of God as a loving and merciful. I do not have all the answers I would like to have regarding Chet's anomalies, but I am sure that God did not do it.

Chet Says: I'm often asked if I've ever questioned God. Hasn't everyone? Doesn't that make us human? A preacher and friend of mine, Rusty Tugman, once said something in a sermon that sums up my thoughts on the matter. After months of anguish over losing a 5-day old baby, Rusty came to the conclusion that he would never hear a satisfying answer to the question of "Why?" while he was on this earth. No one could provide him an answer that would quell his thirst for why this had happened. Instead, it's time to stop laying blame, and time to start figuring out where do we go from here.

I've said before that if I truly believed that God caused my physical deformities, I would not choose to worship him. I have heard suggestions before that I was born this way so that I could show the world how a Christian deals with a disability. How cruel! Anyone who would say that has never lived in my shoes, or they would know better. I think the world needs answers…and I choose to not have that same need.

So, I was born this way to show the world how a Christian deals with disabilities? NO! I try to show the world how a Christian deals with disabilities because I happen to have been born this way. There's a very big difference.

3

A LOT OF HELP
FROM OUR FRIENDS

God has promised to be with us in life in Matthew 28:20 and
Hebrews 13:5-6. I do not understand all of the ways He
helps us, but I am sure we found an inner strength I did not
know we had. Most obviously, God helped us through people, many people.

Judy's mother was already with us for the anticipated birth of her fifteenth grandchild. While we were at the hospital for the birth, she waited with our good friends, the Campbells, who were to bring her, Randy, and Jennifer to the hospital when I called. The Campbells were great that first night and a hundred nights after that. Mom Sims was the marvel. She was well into her 70s at the time of Chet's birth, and seemed to be in good health. She worked hard to keep us balanced emotionally. She took care of Randy and Jennie, and loved Chet more than she would have if he had had no problems. Judy's sisters, Ruth Green and Mildred Rucker, took turns staying us. Two of her brothers, Roy Sims and Marvin Sims, and Marvin's wife, Dot, came for visits to try to lift us.

Ruth didn't get to sleep much while she was with us helping. A mockingbird was nesting in a small tree outside her bedroom window, and it sang all night. Unfortunately, the bird did not sing her to sleep. While Mildred was with us, the furnace caught on fire and burned all the wires. We had to call the fire department in the middle of the night. We were able to stay in the house since only the wiring had been destroyed. However, since we didn't have a central heating unit any more, we all slept in the den on the floor, and I kept the fireplace blazing through the night. The mockingbird and the fire were small issues compared to the weight of the problem we felt.

My sister and her husband, Pat and John McCarley, came to try to help. They started a tradition that proved immensely beneficial throughout many years. They would come and spend Christmas with us, or we would spend it with them. They called once or twice a week for years. I am glad I didn't have to pay their phone bill. All of our brothers and sisters gave us money to help with the many expenses.

When I told the Airline Drive Church of Christ about Chet, they immediately surrounded us with their love and help. They cleaned the house and cooked our food. They helped with Randy and Jennifer, especially during that first week when I spent most of my time at the hospital.

Jim Brigham heard me announce Chet's birth to the church on the morning after his birth. Jim met me at the door of the church building to say, "We can help!" Jim worked for the Caddo-Bossier Association for Retarded Citizens, known as C-BARC. I quickly explained that there was no indication that Chet had any mental problems. Just as quickly, Jim explained that they had other programs, including occupational therapy and physical therapy. We had our first help! Someone knew what we could do immediately.

Throughout Chet's life, we have felt that we did not know the distant future. When he was a little child, we began to feel depressed when we tried to think of his adult years. While we did not know what we could do for the distant future, we always knew what to do each day. We tried to do what we knew to do each day, and let the future take care of itself. We decided to ask, "Is there really any other way for anyone to face life? Does anyone know the distant future?"

C-BARC's Occupational Therapist was a marvel. We felt encouraged when we saw her work with Chet. The Orthopedist had told us that Chet would learn to use his feet like we use our hands, and we began to get a glimpse of this possibility when we watched the OT work. Chet began attending C-Barc at three months of age, and they continued to help until he was two years and eight months old.

Others Helped Too

Dr. Clinton McAlister was our local orthopedist, and he was the best in the city in our opinion. He invited us to let him send a lady to visit us in the hospital. She and her husband had given birth to a daughter about one year prior to Chet's birth, and that daughter was born with no arms or legs. After her visit, we felt like we were not alone. A few weeks later, she and Judy took their babies and went to a local McDonald's. This was Judy's first outing with Chet. Today, Judy laughs about the shock people must have felt when they saw two armless babies.

We soon joined an organization of parents of handicapped children. We heard their stories, and began to realize that our situation was not as bad as what some others faced. We began to use an expression to one another after hearing someone else's story. We would look at one another, and one of us would say, "I wouldn't want to trade places with them."

Next Came the Atlanta Trips

Dr. McAlister referred us to Dr. Richard King, a world-renowned specialist in Atlanta, Georgia. He had treated several patients with conditions similar to Chet's. Once again, the future began to look brighter when we found someone who knew what we were facing and what we could do. Dr. King was the first to tell us that Chet would walk. That news was some of the best we had received since Chet's birth. However, we began to doubt that he would walk before he did. He was three years when he took his first steps. Today, he needs a wheelchair for extended distances, but he walks, runs, wrestles, jumps on a trampoline, and almost anything else he wants to do. When Dr. King said that Chet would walk, he probably did not realize how well Chet would get around. We had to travel to Atlanta every few months, and that was expensive. My sister and her husband, Jan and Richard Craig, lived in Atlanta, and they helped with transportation and lodging. They would interrupt their schedules and take care of us any time we needed to come to Atlanta.

Dr. King wanted us to try prostheses for Chet's legs. These were designed to bring him up to the height of his peers. In August, 1983, J. E. Hanger, Inc. prepared a set of "legs" for Chet at a cost of $4,039, and our insurance company refused to help. We worked with these prostheses for about two years, but most of the time they proved to be frustration for Chet and us. Then, when Dr. King saw Chet on another trip to his Atlanta office, he announced that Chet had rejected the prostheses. He explained that rejection is determined not by a conscious decision on the part of the patient, but by whether the prosthesis helps or hinders. The prostheses took away Chet's confidence, and therefore, the doctor said that Chet rejected them. Later, we went through a similar experience with bilateral myoelectric arms. The Shriners in Shreveport graciously provided these prostheses for Chet. Chet said that they were hot, heavy, awkward, and slow. He was glad each time our exercise session was over, and they were taken off. Chet was elated when Dr. King told us to "put them in a closet and forget them." He said that Chet could learn to use the arms so well that he could put on a show before a television audience, but that Chet would take them off as soon as he got home and use what he came with. Today, he does use his feet to type, write, play computer games, and in any other way most people use their hands. I look at these efforts to introduce Chet to prosthetics as giving him every opportunity to make informed choices. I do not feel that we tried to force him to become something that he is not, but that we went to great lengths to give him the chance to make good choices for his own life.

What Would We Have Done Without "Nanny?"

Chris Webster, a member of the church where I preached, told us before Chet was born and before we knew of any anomalies that she wanted to fill the role of grandmother for this new baby. My mother had died three years before Chet's birth, and Judy's mother lived a thousand miles away. After Chet's birth, Chris seemed to want even more than ever to fill that role. She was one of the ladies who helped at our house. Also, she started taking Chet home with her very early in his life. Since she lived only a few blocks away, she could be there in minutes when we called. And call we did! Soon, Chris was taking Chet to her house almost every weekend for a night and sometimes two. Her husband soon got into the role of grandfather, and is, to this day, "Pops." The Webster's four adult children began to treat Chet like a family member, and their children refer to Chet as their cousin.

Carl Webster, in earlier years, had been a Sunday school teacher and church song leader, but by 1980, Carl had quit attending church. When Chet was less than two years old, he began to ask Carl to go to church with him and Nanny. Carl could not refuse Chet. Soon, that fire for the Lord stirred in Carl's heart, and he became strong in the Lord again. He has since served as one of the leaders in the church. Before he could know what he was doing, Chet had his first influence for the Lord. Carl has repaid Chet for his good influence many times over and in many ways.

Thank God for Cousins

Joe and Bobbie McDoniel, cousins, lived in Bossier City, and were already close to us before Chet's birth. In fact, they had filled the role of grandparents for Jennifer, born in 1972. I was able to lean on Joe and talk to him anytime I needed an outlet, and Bobbie was always glad to take care of Chet. Her special service was caring for babies. She often worked in the nursery at church. They stayed especially close and were of great benefit during our time in the hospital.

Wow, the Costs!

Those trips to Atlanta to see Dr. King were expensive. He did not charge any more than most other doctors, but the travel was tough. I made some of the airline trips without Judy because of the cost. I could carry Chet, bags, and prostheses, and at that point, I was stronger emotionally, also. Sometimes, we traveled by van, but that took both money and time.

At age three, Chet needed a powered wheelchair. His first wheelchair cost $6,544.75. It had power brakes, heavy-duty electric motors and brakes, and a powered leg lift for Chet to be able to get into the chair. It provided a great sense of freedom for Chet, and it lasted for about ten years. Powered wheelchairs require vans with lifts, and the expenses continued.

Judy was part of a neighborhood ladies' study group called, "The Potpourri Club," and they donated the money for the lift to go in our new van. The state of Louisiana paid for Chet's new powered chair. Art Cook was a member of the Airline Drive Church of Christ and an insurance agent with Great Southern. Art started collecting money for Chet, and his efforts paid for many of the trips to Atlanta. He fought for Chet to have life insurance, and it was a fight. Art said that Chet was one of the first severely handicapped persons in the nation to be insured. Kind people and churches sent money, and it was desperately needed. Several of the benefactors sent their gifts to Chet, and we were careful to keep those gifts in a saving account for him.

I don't know how we could have made it through the early years without the Airline Drive Church of Christ. They wept with us, and prayed for us. They gave us whatever time was needed to take care of Chet. They gave most of the money that Art raised. Through the first twelve years of Chet's life, many of those church members befriended us. Bob Mosley took Chet for a plane ride. First, Junior Hollis and later, Van Hutches welded Chet's wheelchair when it broke, and it seemed to break often. Guy Clawson let him work in the benevolence room at the church.

Chet was never bashful or slow to try new things. Soon, after Chet got his first wheelchair, he was sailing around the church parking lot. I saw him stop and look at the ball field. Rains had left the field muddy and even covered in part by water. When I saw him look at the water, I yelled, "No," but Chet did not hear. As fast as the chair would run, Chet ploughed into the mud. The chair sank down, and its wheels began to spin. Troy Freeman, my best friend, almost collapsed laughing and then, waded into the mud with me to help pull the chair and Chet out of the mud. Troy and Carolyn helped a hundred times after that. Since Troy and I directed camp together at the Ark-La-Tex Christian Camp, he even had additional occasions to pull Chet's chair out of the mud.

These friends helped us treat Chet like any other kid. We have often felt that having a handicapped child with a "poor me" attitude would be even worse than the actual handicap. We told Chet that the world does not owe him anything that it does not owe everyone else. We wanted Chet to do for himself whatever he could do, and have a full life. He could not play tee ball, but he got to coach first base. He was a Cub Scout and a Webelo. Martin Faktor, also from the church, helped me with a Cub Scout Den and later, he helped me become a scoutmaster. Chet got to go to camp because the counselors that we used at the Ark-La-Tex Christian Camp worked extra when he was in their cabin, and they all seemed to want him in their cabin. All these friends loved Chet, helped when they could, but they excelled at letting Chet be just another kid.

Chris Webster likes to tease me about my estimate of interest and support for Chet at his second birthday. Chris told me that she was planning a birthday party at the church building for Chet, and she had reserved the room that would hold about 400 people. I told Chris that she was thinking too big. I said, "Chris, not everyone loves Chet like you do." Still, I appreciated her efforts and agreed to help get Chet there. The room was full. There were far too many gifts for a two-year old. People were extremely gracious and happy in their celebration of his birthday.

In 1988, we got a glimpse of how Chet had accepted that philosophy of life. A local television station did a special report on Chet. They did a great job, and Chet looked like a hero. In the interview, the reporter asked Chet if the teachers gave him any special considerations. Chet answered, "If one of them tells me, 'I'll give you a few less problems to work than the others so your foot doesn't get too tired,' I tell her, 'No, I'll take all of them.'" We told him to hold on to that attitude. He learned to do what he could for himself, and we are deeply grateful for help from our friends.

4

IT'S OFF TO SCHOOL WE GO

Chet started going to C-Barc for occupational therapy and for physical therapy when he was just a few months old, and we continued faithfully taking him for his appointments. We knew that we needed help, and these folks had some ideas. We could see the results of their work almost immediately, especially that of the exceptional occupational therapist, Judi Vestal.

When Chet was two years and eight months old, C-Barc told us that we needed to enroll him in their all day school, for five days each week. They reasoned that he needed a major head start, and he needed extra training to develop good co-ordination with his feet to learn to accomplish small muscle jobs. Judy struggled hard with this decision. She felt that he was just too young to start school and be away from her all day everyday. She agreed to give it a try, and within a couple of weeks, Chet loved it and looked forward to being with his friends. A new problem arose after two years in the C-Barc school. Chet was still only four. He was too young for kindergarten and too old for C-Barc's program. The Airline Drive Church of Christ had started a preschool program under the direction of Guy Clawson. We enrolled Chet, and he had a great year. The C-Barc school had been close, but taking Chet to school in the building where I had my office was especially nice. Still, these three years proved to be a difficult time for Judy emotionally. Maybe it was simply that Chet was our last child, but I think the bigger issue was his handicap. She felt that she should have been permitted more time with him at home to build that mother-child early bonding and for time to get the same early training that she gave the older two children. Chet needed training that we could not personally provide, and that was difficult to accept.

The Battle Over 504

After the two years at C-BARC and one at the Airline Drive Preschool, Chet was ready for kindergarten in the Bossier

Parish School System. Randy and Jennie had attended Apollo Elementary School, only two blocks from our house. Judy had taught there, filling in for teachers. We, naturally, anticipated Chet going there, close to home and with people that we knew and trusted. The coordinator for Special Education for the Bossier Parish School District, Donnalee Ammons, broke our hearts when she told us that Chet would have to ride a special bus for three miles to Kerr Elementary because it was the "504 location." "504" was an idea that children who needed adaptation in their educational setting should all be placed together for the convenience of the providers. Other handicapped children from across the city were bussed there, and this five-year-old with his wheelchair could attend only this school. Chet already had been going to Kerr a couple of days each week for occupational therapy, physical therapy, and adaptive physical education with Dr. Wesley Cragin who loved Chet like he was her own child. Still, the thought that he might have to go to school there broke our hearts afresh.

Since Judy is a teacher, she knew to plead for "inclusion." We went back to one of Judy's friends at the "Potpourri Study Club." She was on the school board for the Parish, and believed in inclusion. She and another board member talked to the principal of Apollo Elementary School, John Castore, and they thrilled us beyond words when they called to say that Chet would be welcome at our neighborhood school. That second School Board member was in charge of finding jobs for senior citizens that would then be paid by the federal government. He simply hired two of those older ladies to attend Chet's classes with him, one from early morning until noon and the other from noon until school was out. Soon, Chet needed only help with lunch and a couple of restroom stops, and only one of the ladies worked with him, from 10 until 2 each day.

Mr. Castore and his teachers were pleased to work with us, and Chet loved school. We had learned about I.E.P. (Individual Evaluation Programs) when the school district first began to provide services, but now that Chet was in Apollo, I.E.P. meetings became regular. To the credit of Apollo Elementary School these always seemed positive and encouraging. The records of those meetings show in detail the adaptations for the classroom and the plans of Dr. Cragin and Suzanne Lee, an occupational therapist, who worked with Chet for years.

Chet's first grade teacher wrote on an I.E.P. report in August, 1986, "Chet amazes me with such a positive attitude toward himself and others." Of course, there is the note that asks us to remind him to "stay on task, and listen to instruction better." He liked to make sounds (somewhat like humming) while he was working. This had to go! Still the oldest report card we have shows an "A" in each of the two graded subjects, math and reading. In fact, Chet was soon placed in the gifted and talented program. Throughout his school years, Chet has made good grades and has participated well in classes.

One of the first successful stories of Chet's physical efforts came from a coloring contest. "Sesame Street on Stage" was scheduled to appear in Shreveport when Chet was in the second grade. The local newspaper announced a coloring contest and promised free tickets to the Sesame Street performance to the winners. Of course, Chet wanted to color a picture. I suppose that every student in the class participated. I don't remember how many winners there were, but Chet was one of the winners. I was totally surprised, but glad to take the family to Sesame Street.

When Chet was in the fifth grade, he was invited to participate in a "Dressage" program. A local farm had miniature horses that were trained to pull a racing surrey. Chet and other handicapped students learned to drive the horses, groom them, and relate to them. Chet fell in love with a horse named "Twelve", and we have great pictures of Chet driving Twelve. Recently, as I was helping Chet move from our house to his apartment, I found the certificate of completion for the Dressage Course. Chet was in a "throw-it-out mood," but he smiled at the certificate and said, "I think I'll keep that."

Like most kids, Chet liked recess. He had a lot of friends, and with his powered chair, he could keep up with most of them. When he was in fourth grade, Judy paid a visit to the school. When she started to leave, she saw Chet on the "monkey bars." He had climbed about six feet off the ground and was holding on with his arm, which was about two inches long. Judy had stopped the car and started to go get him down when she realized that teachers standing near seemed comfortable with his climb. When he came home that day, Judy asked him about his climb. He explained that he climbed up that high everyday. "You can see a long way from that height," he explained. We got his pediatrician to tell him that climbing like that was unwise.

When Chet started to attend Apollo, one of us walked with him to school or near the school. In bad weather, I would take him, chair and all, in the van. After he got a little older, we would walk along the street portion of the trip with him, but just watch as he crossed the field to his school. Eventually, we let him go on his own. Friends were on their bikes, and Chet was in the middle of the group in his chair. He was Mr. Independent, and that is who he has always wanted to be.

Maybe the hardest part of Chet going to school was not the physical aspect, the fight over "504," or any I.E.P., but just letting go. We knew that eventually Chet would need to be as independent as possible, and so we turned loose little by little. Turning loose hurts! We hurt so he would not hurt so much later in life. Today, we are glad we pushed him (or let him move) toward independence, but at the time, it just hurt.

Chet Says: I laugh sometimes when looking back on my early independent personality. Now, more than ever, I am an independent adult, but stories that I've heard of my early childhood have made me realize that it all had to start somewhere. In fact, I also think it's funny that my parents were so surprised by my attitude. After all, they were the ones who were constantly telling me that I was no different than anyone else. I listened to them, and determined that if I was no different than anyone else, then I should be able to do anything that someone else with arms could do.

I am also so thankful for "inclusion." Recently, I got to speak at a large gathering of K-12 educators discussing inclusion. I told them how important that theme was to me as being in a classroom with other students taught me so much, and I would have missed out on that social interaction had I been secluded with others who looked like me. I dare say that my being in a regular classroom helped the other students learn about disability. After speaking to the group of teachers and administrators, one teacher came up to me and apologized. She told me that she had been dreading inclusion because of the extra work that it would mean for her. She said that the presentation had reminded her that all children are to be loved and educated no matter what situation they are in. I love the attitude, and I am so thankful for forward-thinking minds in the Bossier Parish school system in 1985.

5

FEATS OF DARING DO

When Chet was only a few months old, he began to use his feet much as our other children had used their hands. We never knew if he started using his feet because of the training of the occupational therapists or if it was simply natural to him. At the time of his first Christmas, he was almost one year old. He liked the Christmas tree, and his brother and sister soon had him playing at the lower branches and decorations. He lay on his back and kicked at everything he could reach. Then, he grabbed the garland rope with his foot and pulled hard. Randy caught the tree just as it started to fall on top of Chet. We thought that we might do well to stay close if he was going to play with the tree, but we were happy to see his ability to use his feet.

When Chet was only a few months old, we started those trips to see Dr. Richard King in Atlanta. On one of those visits, Dr. King was telling us what we should expect in the future. He causally said, "Now, when Chet begins to walk, he will..." That is as far as he got with that sentence when we interrupted him. Strangely, I remember that I was the startled one who interrupted to say, "What did you say?" Judy remembers herself being the one who stopped Dr. King. We were both startled, and both of us wanted to know if the Doctor said what he meant to say. Poor Dr. King didn't realize what the surprise was all about. He looked a little blank and replied, "I said, 'When he begins to walk, he will...'" Again, that is as far as we let him speak. We asked, "You mean, Chet will walk?" "Oh, yes!" Dr. King answered. Then, he embarrassedly asked, "Has no one told you that he will walk?" No one had, and that news was unbelievable. In fact, we asked Dr. King, "But how? Without bone structure to support himself, how can he walk?" He explained that Chet would develop enough muscle to support himself for short distances. He added that he would walk by swiveling his hips. It was almost too good to be true.

When he was well past his first birthday, Chet learn to stand, and with help he could move his feet, but the promise of seeing him walk began to seem empty. I suppose both of us had given up on Dr. King's promise. One day when he was three, he had spent most of the day with Chris Webster, "Nanny." When we came to pick him up, Chris had huge tears in her eyes, as she greeted us with the news, "Chet walked." We were listening intently to her recounting of the story, when Chet announced, "I did like this." He leaned forward and stood, and then took three steps into the arms of his mother. Soon, he was demonstrating his new skill to everyone who would watch.

Again the therapists came to our rescue. All children fall when they are beginning to walk, but Chet had no way of catching himself or breaking his fall. The OT taught him to lower his shoulder and roll. It has to happen quickly, but he learned the trick quickly, too. Still, today, if he stumbles, he tucks his shoulder in, rolls, and comes back up on his feet so quickly that he hardly misses a step.

But Too Daring

Later in this third year, Chet got that new powered wheel-chair. It was unusually heavy, and was faster that any wheelchair I have seen. Chet liked both its power and speed. As soon as he got the chair, we went to the church building and let him practice in the multipurpose room. Soon, he was going full speed everywhere he went. Several children used the three hallways in the back of the church building for running and playing. Now, with his wheelchair, Chet could join them. Then, the day came when Chet was driving full speed down one of those halls in a game of chase, and he was looking back over his shoulder at someone running after him. He ran right though a sheet-rock wall. Our good friend, Troy Freeman, could fix anything. He laughed, told me that he would repair the wall, and told me not to be too hard on Chet. I wanted to repair the wall, but he insisted that he would do it. Maybe he insisted on repairing the wall because he knew what my repair job would look like.

When our children were little, they often went to the office with me. We kept toys in a certain section of my cabinets. One day when Chet was about six, he and a friend who was a couple of years older had a skateboard at the church building. The wheel chair ramp at the rear of the building was great for building up speed for any skate boarder who came by. Soon, Chet came to get me to watch him on the skateboard. He would lie down on his side, use his shorter leg to propel himself down the ramp, and he would sail across the parking lot. I thought it was great, though dangerous. However, Judy came by the building that day, and she put a stop to the activity immediately. She asked, "And what happens when you fall off, face first, and six inches from pavement?"

Since I directed a session for the 4th, 5th, and 6th graders at the Ark-La-Tex Christian Camp each year, Chet started going as a pre-camper when he was only six or seven. He loved camp, and moved into a cabin of boys as soon as he was old enough. He required some help, but several of the cabin counselors and most of his friends were willing to supply whatever help he needed. Then, came the year of the rain, and that powerful wheelchair met its match in the mud of the Ark-La-Tex Camp. Chet's friends quickly learned that the wheels would spin and throw mud like an automobile in mud. One day, the ground was soft everywhere, and the rain was gently falling. Chet was moving as fast as he could as he made his way from the bathhouse back toward his cabin. Then, the chair mired down in the mud and stopped. His counselor had just showered and put on dry, clean clothes. He shouted to Chet that he was coming to help. However, he got behind the chair to push, and told Chet to give the chair all the power he could. In a flash, the chair spun the wheels fast and threw an unbelievable amount of mud and water on those clean clothes. Fortunately, Troy Freeman, assistant director, and I were watching from inside the main building were we could hide behind a wall as we doubled up laughing. I did not laugh as much when I got the chair back home and started trying to rid the chair of the dried mud, especially in the groves on the main drive pulleys.

"Nanny" put a large plastic playhouse in the grandchildren's room at her house. It was designed for children to be able to walk into, but the boys soon decided that climbing on top of it would be more fun. When Nanny went in to check on the children, she found Chet on top of the playhouse with the others. However, he had slipped down the roof and was barely hanging on, having gotten one foot on something that stopped his slide. When, she lifted him off, he said, "When I started sliding, I knew I was dead meat." We still can't figure how he got on top of it.

Trampoline jumping was a favorite activity for Randy and Jennifer. Even Judy and I got on the trampoline when no one was looking. Both Randy and Jennie were quite good at doing front flips and back flips. Since they liked it so much, Chet was soon on the trampoline with them. He sat down, and they bounced him in the air, at first. Soon, he was springing from his seat to a full jump. He often went around the trampoline very fast, and sometimes even bounced himself off and onto the ground, three feet below. He never hurt himself badly. After he was accustomed to being on the trampoline, I built a stepladder so he could get on it without help. He and his friends spent many hours bouncing away.

Chet always loved to play catch. He would lie on his back and with one foot, or sometimes with both; he would rock back and throw a ball or a beanbag across the room. Early in his life, he could catch quite well, too. He could carry on this "catch" until he wore down everyone in the room. We moved to the Pipeline Rd. Church of Christ when Chet was eleven. He and I moved in with one of the elders and his wife, Dr. and Mrs. John Bailey, while Judy stayed behind to sell the house and finish her job. The Baileys had the singles from church over for a devotional on a Sunday evening. Chet threw a small beanbag to everyone in the room. Each time a new person walked into the den, he would call out, "Catch," and heave the beanbag in their direction. Then, Ron walked in. He called for Chet to throw to him, but I don't think he ever saw the beanbag. Chet caught him square in the face, and with the surprise, it almost knocked him down. I had the difficult task of correcting Chet while trying to keep a straight face. I don't think Ron thought it was funny, but everyone else in the room did.

Chet was in the sixth grade, when we moved to Bedford, Texas. He got to be in on the choice of our house and his school. We narrowed the choice to three schools and searched for just the right house. We chose a house on Rolling Meadows Drive just down the street from Spring Gardens Elementary School. Yes, I said, "down the street." Rolling Meadows runs down a sloping hill for about two blocks before the ground is level. That first powered chair would run eight miles an hour on level ground, and it had no limit switch when going down a hill. One day, a neighbor claimed that he clocked Chet going down that hill at 20 miles an hour. We told Chet that he had to slow down for safety, but I think he soon forgot our warning. Judy was not sad to learn that his next chair had a limit switch that applied brakes anytime he got faster than eight miles per hour.

When Chet was eleven, I took him to a Halloween party.

The party was put on by some teenagers, and they enlisted Chet's help. Chet was unknown to the younger children and to some of those of his own age. He hid under a table, and children were brought in where the "mad surgeon" was ready to operate. The teenagers told the children that the surgeon would cut off their arms and legs, and then announced that the kids could see his last patient. At that point, Chet jumped out covered in ketchup or something red, and scared the poor children too badly. They had to adjust their stunt after the first small group came through. Chet thought that scene was hilarious.

Chet was an adult before he told his mother about the "Creamora fire." While we were out one evening, a group of teenage boys were at the house. The boys had heard that Creamora would burn, and make a beautiful sparkling, slow burning fire. They took turns sprinkling small amounts of Creamora into a small fire on our back porch. However, something went wrong. The lid came off, and the entire can of Creamora caught fire. The boy who was holding the can of Creamora threw toward the ceiling to get it out of his hand. Suddenly the entire ceiling of the porch lit up. The boys scrambled for the water hose and put the fire out. When I asked about the black on the porch ceiling, Chet told me part of the story. I don't suppose I knew just how close we came to tragedy until I heard the story as he told his mother, when "the statute of limitations" had run out.

He Wanted to Ski

 The teenagers from church went to Colorado every year to ski. Since Chet was a part of the group, he wanted to go. By this time, we had learned to step back and let him do what he thought he could. Also, the ski resorts have developed programs for handicapped skiers. Still, I could not imagine how Chet could ski. He sits in a chair (bucket) that is mounted to two skis. He is tethered to an instructor by a loose rope. Chet's job is to maintain balance and to turn from side to side, leaning as he turns, just like any skier. He found no difficulty in this new sport. He loves it. Yes, he fell, but he was ready to try again each time. In one day, he graduated from the beginner slopes to the green runs, and eventually to blues. One day, probably before he was ready, he saw a slope called "Chet Run." He had to try it, and his instructors reluctantly agreed. They explained to him that they had never taken a "bi-skier" down this run before. They were moving fast when they approached a jump point. Chet chose to go directly over it. He called home to announce, "Today, I got air for the first time." Chet has been skiing many times since then, and can't wait to go again.

Perhaps more dangerous than the actual skiing, was the fun of riding an inner tube down a slope. Chet had a great friendship with Stephen and Jonathan Robertson, who were a few years older and loved adventure. Stephen and Chet got on one of the large inner tubes. Stephen ran, pushing the inner tube, as fast as he could and eventually jumped on with Chet. They flew down the slope, and then, could not stop at the bottom of the run. They ploughed through everything and everyone in their path, yelling and laughing as they went. An embankment finally stopped their forward motion. All you can hear on the video of the event is Chet, laughing all the way.

I am sure that we do not know all the dangerous stunts Chet pulled. We don't know everything our older two children did, so why should we think we know everything Chet did? Letting him go, and letting him be as normal as his body would let him was hard. I have heard Judy say, "Sometimes, I just have to turn and walk away. I must let him do what he thinks he can." Maybe every parent has trouble turning loose, but when a child has physical limits, the job is even tougher. Still, we are convinced that we had to work, early in his life, to help him be as independent and self-sufficient as he could be. Building that spirit of independence meant that he had to take some risks, just as do children who are physically whole, and that Mom (and Dad) had to gently untie the apron strings and let him go.

Chet Says: Wow, what memories! They are all very true stories, and while some of them illustrate a clear lack of judgment on my part, the stories all tell of one thing: Independence. I never have, nor will I ever view myself as handicapped. The word itself throws up so many roadblocks that keep people from living happy, full lives. My lack of arms has never deterred me from living out my dreams. My body may look different to others, but it is normal for me. So, I got into just as much trouble as the average kid because that's what I was…a kid. I wasn't a "kid without arms"…I was just a "kid."

It would have been very easy for my parents to hold me back and "protect" me due to my disability, but they chose not to. Instead they, along with friends, taught me to enjoy life and never to allow my perceived limitations to become actual limitations. I am grateful for being allowed to experience life instead of being sheltered. I believe that is a choice every parent has to make. I know that the time will come for me to let go of my own children and allow them to fly on their own. I'm sure it will be difficult, but it has to be done.

And, dad's right, they don't know all of the crazy things I have done…

6

THE GOOD, THE BAD,
THE UGLY, AND
THE BEAUTIFUL

Over the years of Chet's life, we have faced many different reactions to his handicap and to us as a family. Some of these have been great and encouraging, and some thoughtless and cruel. Many people have not known how to respond, and some that have tried to say the right thing said exactly the wrong thing.

The Ugly

When Chet was about one year old, Judy was carrying him on her hip into a fast food restaurant. A stranger that met them in the doorway boldly raised Chet's sleeve to get a better look, and asked, "What the hell happened to him, lady?" Judy handled that situation better than I would have, but she was deeply hurt. That response is one that I would call "the ugly." Maybe the title of this chapter should have had another category for that fellow. Maybe it should be "The Good, the Bad, the Ugly, the Stupid, and the Beautiful."

Three times that I know about, a boy has wanted to fight Chet. The first one of those incidents happened while he was in school in Apollo Elementary. Chet laughed as he told us about the event. A fellow student got mad and him and took a swing at him. Chet ducked that swing and before the boy could strike again, three students and two teachers were on him. He was a friend who made a mistake, and the incident was over and forgotten for Chet. Still, his mother and I wondered what he would be able to do to defend himself.

Lull Hankings who built Chet's first chair, told us to teach him to use his chair as a weapon if he was attacked. Lull had been confined to a wheelchair for many years. Just before our conversation, Lull had been able to throw a would-be thief to the ground. The thief, then, ran away.

Chet found the occasion to use his chair as a weapon when he was in junior high school. One student often spoke of wanting to "beat up" Chet. The two boys often exchanged words, but no blows. Then, one day, the boy declared that this was the day he would fight Chet. Chet agreed to fight him, and he ordered, "Alright, get out of your chair." Chet answered, "No way, I am going to use the chair, and I will break your ankle." The agitator thought for a minute, replied, "You are not worth it," and walked away. As usual, a crowd had gathered for the fight, and they applauded boldly. I gave the usual warning about never being the aggressor, but I was pleased with the way he had handled the situation. Since his mother is a school teacher, she thought the situation should have been handled differently.

The third occasion was the most unbelievable because the man who threatened Chet was in college. This time, Chet took the matter to the police who promised to help if needed. Maybe the man came to senses because he wrote only one foul letter threatening Chet.

The Bad

During the early weeks of Chet's life, a few well- intentioned people told us that God chose us for this "special child." Their comments varied slightly, but they were all suggesting that God had a limb deficient child in heaven to send to earth, and He needed a family with a special measure of love and strength to take care of this child. He chose us. Wow! Thanks!

While there are some people who believe that children exist in heaven before coming to this earth, we do not. Further, if God did have a "baby bank" in heaven, the thought that one of those babies was incomplete presents a God that we can't find in the Bible. Further yet, if God did send a handicapped child from His "baby bank" to us because we were a special family, God made a mistake. We did not have the strength to handle the situation in exemplary fashion. No, we never failed Chet, but our level of strength had to be aided by the Lord many times.

Even today, good people trying to say something helpful, tell us that Chet is a blessing. Chet is a blessing. His body is in- complete. His incomplete body is not what makes him a blessing. He has overcome his limits, and Chet is a whole person. Still, his body is not whole, and it is not a blessing.

Both of us, sometimes together, sometimes individually, have stood, watching Chet while he was sleeping, and wept. There was a time when that weeping was beneficial to us. Eventually, we learned not to just stand and look. As Chet would say, "It is time to get on with life."

I mentioned in chapter two that one lady that we knew years ago, wrote us when Chet was born to tell us that God sent us a handicapped child as a punishment for some sin in our lives. She did not presume to identify the sin, but she was sure that we could if we would. She pled with us to confess the sin and get it out of our lives. We barely knew the lady who wrote, but her message added to our burden. We chose not to write her.

Another lady, whom we barely knew, wanted us to take Chet to a faith healer. That lady saw Chet and me at a workshop when Chet was nineteen years old. She told us that for about two dozen years she had been expecting a miracle that would cure her son's problems. She added that as soon as she got her miracle, she would start praying for us to have one. I guess she believes that God can only entertain one request at a time.

We tried to be kind to her, but we were both uncomfortable. When we got the chance to talk, Chet announced, "I don't want her miracle. I have a life. I wouldn't know what to do with arms if I had them." I suggested to Chet that that lady spends her days wishing that her life were different. We spend our days serving God with what we have.

The Good

Teachers in junior high and high school have told us that Chet's attitude and outlook on life have been an inspiration to them. One teacher said, "When I am having a tough day, and then, I meet Chet in the hall, my spirits rise." She added something like, "If Chet can be happy as he goes down the hall in a wheelchair, my problems should not be allowed to keep me down."

Chet has spoken to a few classes about how he gets along in life. However, he did not like that job while he was in school. It called attention to his handicap, which he chooses to ignore. Also, he has refused some requests simply because he is always busy.

Every time Chet has been before an audience, usually singing, he has received great support from friends and from the audience. For example, he led singing at church recently. Church members couldn't say enough about how uplifting the worship was. Judy and I wondered how many compliments he would have received if he has not been limb deficient. He did an outstanding job, and he and I work well together. Still, we thought that part of the lift that people received came from the fact that he has the courage to stand before people and lead despite the fact that he has no arms.

When Chet was in high school, he learned Garth Brooks' "The River." The song carries a great message encouraging people to do what they can. Chet performed the song in four or five settings, and received a standing ovation every time. Undoubtedly the song has a great message, but combine that message with Chet's physical person, singing it well, and the audiences were deeply moved.

When Chet was in high school, he worked at Six Flags. Soon, he became a ride operator and shift supervisor. One day, he was in charge of a shift at "Flashback," and was in the booth driving the ride. On this ride, as on several others, the handicapped riders could come up the exit ramp and board the ride on the exit side rather than waiting in the long line. Six Flags started that procedure because the queue lines are narrow and often have stairs leading to the ride. An able bodied woman saw a handicapped person get this advantage, and she started to complain. She had waited in the long line, and she didn't think that it was fair that the handicapped person did not have to wait as long as she had. She fussed loudly at the young ride attendants. When they could not calm her down, they asked if she would like to speak to their supervisor. Of course, she said that she definitely wanted to speak to their supervisor. They waved to Chet, who could only be seen from the shoulders up from that position on the platform. He secured the ride, and climbed down from the booth. When he walked into the small crowd gathered for the complaint, his crew announced, "Chet, this lady has a complaint to take up with you." He smiled and asked what he could do for her. She paused only briefly before she responded, "Oh, never mind." He had not heard the previous conversation, but he saw that his crew was fighting hard not to burst out laughing. He was in a hurry to start the ride again, but later, when he learned the full story, he loved it.

When Chet was in high school, he loved to go football games. He usually sat with friends in the stands, but he used his powered wheelchair to get into the stadium and near the seats. One night, near the end of a game, I went to pick him. I walked into the stadium, this time to check the score. Just as I rounded a corner, I saw a presumptuous junior high student sit down in Chet's chair and start trying the controls. Before I was close enough to say anything to him, I heard a loud voice order, "Get out of that chair." The voice had come from a large high school student. The boy in the chair challenged, "It ain't your chair, is it?" The reply came back sharply and loud, "No, but it belongs to a friend of mine, and if I catch you in it again, I am going to beat your face in." The lad quickly left the chair, especially since the older student was closing in on the spot quickly. I stepped back and just let the older student handle the situation. Chet has always had friends who looked after him and his needs.

Throughout his school years, Chet's friends handled books for him. They opened doors, and helped his chair if it was hung. He always had someone who was willing to help him with lunch, and it was usually a pretty girl. During his sophomore year in high school, Darren Morrison became his lab partner and good friend. Darren was on the wrestling team of the school, muscled and well over six feet tall, and they looked as different as two could. Darren had a pickup truck with 36-inch tires, and the two went to lunch off campus every day. Darren carried a step ladder in the back of his truck that Chet could use to get into the cab. He never seemed to mind setting it up for Chet to climb up. They looked different, but in my ways they were alike. Darren proved to be Chet's best friend throughout high school, and their friendship continues to this day.

Chet's high school had an unusually large number of Tongans in it. They stayed together, and some accused them of harassing other students. Chet said that they were nice to him, and a couple of them were his friends. We taught him to treat others with respect, and expect them to respond with respect. Perhaps the fact that he accepted this principle is the reason that he has had several friends from different racial and ethnic backgrounds over the years.

In looking back over the good and the bad we have faced, the good far outweighs the bad. Chet has been an inspiration to many, and he will continue to encourage and lift because of who he is, in spite of having no arms. When I stop and remember the past, the help, friendships, and encouragement we have received from others come to mind. The painful incidents seem so small when compared to the good we have met in life. Often, whether life is beautiful or ugly is determined by how we view the past. We have tried to teach Chet to look for the good, and to be a part of that good.

Chet Says: I remember the phrase, "consider the source." Early on in life, I learned that some people could not seem to help themselves when it came to staring at me. Now, when it is a young child, that's simply curiosity and often avails me of the opportunity to teach the child that God loves everyone no matter what they look like. But, when it is an adult who stares, that's just plain ol' being rude. The phrase "consider the source" came to me in high school, and has helped me immensely when dealing with other peoples' rude behavior. If someone is staring, pointing, or laughing at me (and all three at once, sometimes), I just figure that they have such low self-esteem that the only way they can feel good about themselves is to treat others poorly. I call this, "living a broken life" and I go into more detail on the subject in my book, I'm Not Broken: You Don't Need Arms to Be Happy (www.chetmcdoniel.com). What a sad way to live. However, their rudeness does not get to me as I simply "consider the source." It doesn't make their behavior right, but it does allow me to continue on with a smile.

As my dad mentioned, I've had many more positive reactions than negative ones. I've always felt surrounded and loved by friends and family. Sure, some people are rude, but they are just fleeting moments in my life compared to the true joy of all those who love me. There has been much more "Good" than "Bad" or "Ugly."

7

THE BENEFITS
OF TEXAS

In 1991, I decided to move the family to Bedford, Texas, a suburb of Fort Worth. Chet had just started the sixth grade at Apollo Elementary School in Bossier City, Louisiana. He was established with friends, teachers, neighbors, and the church. Our greatest fear regarding the move was disturbing his world. In fact, I had felt for two years that it was time for me to move to another church. I still loved the Airline Drive Church of Christ, but I thought they needed someone new in the pulpit and that I needed a new work. We had not moved because we feared what the move would do to Chet.

When I announced the move, Chet was unhappy with me. I don't know that he feared a new location. He was just happy where he was. With the help of one of the ladies of the church, he even started a petition to get me to stay. As soon as I heard about the petition, I put a quick stop to it. To our surprise, Chet made the transition easier than anyone else in the family. We soon found some advantages to being in the state of Texas, and we now believe that the move was the best choice we could have made for Chet.

Judy had been back in education for two years, after being a stay-at-home mom for twenty years. We wanted her to stay home for the children, and when Chet arrived with his anomalies, we felt her presence was especially important. When it came time for us to move, she stayed in Bossier City and continued to teach while the Bossier Parish School District graciously looked for a replacement for her. Chet and I moved to Bedford in October, 1991, and I began to preach at the Pipeline Road Church of Christ in Hurst, Texas. He and I stayed with two families for a few weeks while we house hunted, and closed the deal on the chosen house. We had decided that Chet should get to help with choice of schools, and that choice would determine where we lived. Chet and I visited several schools. We liked one near the church build-ing, and the principal seemed especially nice, but the building was not wheelchair accessible. We looked at another school where the principal told me, "You would do well to take him to another school." He rather whispered his advice as if he thought Chet would not hear him. He did not talk to Chet any of the time, only to me. We did go somewhere else, expressly to get to a school with a different principal.

When we looked at Spring Garden Elementary in Bedford, we were met by a loving assistant principal and a gentle outgoing principal. A guide showed us around the nice, accessible building. A pretty girl looked out of a classroom window, waved at Chet and winked at him. I liked the school, and Chet loved the school. His part of the decision was made! We found a house that we liked close to Spring Garden, and soon, Chet was enrolled. When we went to enroll, I explained that Chet had been in the gifted and talented program in Louisiana (LEAP). The principal gently explained that he might not be in Texas because the standards are different in each state. Then, I handed him Chet's academic folder. After a quick glance, he exclaimed, "Oh, get the teacher of gifted students. We have here a child who scored 140 on the ITBS" (Iowa Test of Basic Skills). We enjoyed the seven months Chet spent in that school. He soon found friends. The teachers and administrators were helpful and loving.

The state of Louisiana required each student with special needs to have an "ARD" to develop an "IEP." "ARD" stands for "Admission, Review, and Dismissal," and "IEP" stands for "Individualized Education Program." Chet's first

IEP meeting was on May 20, 1983. We were quite anxious. We had heard horror stories of how schools did not want special needs students and tried to discourage every goal of the parents. I am pleased to say that we never encountered that ugly attitude. We faced some procedural issues that had to be discussed, but we felt that every school Chet attended worked to make his experience pleasant and beneficial.

I felt especially good when Chet had his first ARD meeting in Texas. By this time, we had learned to trust the schools, and Spring Garden Elementary School seemed glad to have Chet. He needed few physical modifications at this point in his life. Of course, he brought a powered wheelchair into the classrooms, and that took considerable space. Desks had to be lowered, and classmates helped with feeding. The gym teacher helped some with restroom, and I tried to be available for extended help. The gym teacher, also, made sure Chet had alternate activities to take the place of any regular activities that he could not do. He soon found out that those were few and far between. The assessment form from an early ARD says regarding Chet:

 *Is a deep thinker
 *Contributes during open discussion
 *Strong comprehension skills
 *Strong problem solving skills
 *Ability to interact with peers
 *Has adapted to his handicap remarkably well
 *Willing to try almost anything

That cooperative spirit that we found at Spring Garden was demonstrated several times at Harwood Junior High School and at Trinity High School. Whatever adaptations Chet needed, he received immediately.

Since his older brother and sister had both played in their school bands, Chet wanted to play the snare drum in junior high. The director thought his ankle was too weak, and told him everyday, "Chet, I doubt you can do this." That was one of the few teachers who ever discouraged him, and Chet soon began to lose interest. I don't think he believed he couldn't, but rather, with that amount of discouragement, Chet decided that he didn't want to play the drums.

At the same time he was also singing in the choir program. The director was helpful and showed confidence in Chet's potential. She gets a lot of the credit for his singing ability today. In high school, he had a knowledgeable choir director, and we arranged for private voice lessons there.

We were pleased with the academic standards of the Hurst-Euless-Bedford school district. I believe Chet would have gotten a good education in the school system of Bossier Parish (Louisiana), and we are especially pleased to have had the benefits of good start in Louisiana and a strong finish in Texas. We soon learned the difference between two programs in HEB schools. In contrast to PEAK in elementary school, PEAK for junior high and high school students simply meant more work. Peak students were called on to turn in more homework and spend more hours per day studying. He braved his way through the program in junior high, but since extensive writing is difficult for Chet, he decided in high school that he did not fit PEAK. He remained classified as an Honor Program student throughout his time in the HEB schools.

The state of Louisiana had helped with the purchase of Chet's first chair, and the chair served us well. However, after nine years, it had gotten to the point that it was not reliable. The shop that sold us the chair had replaced the motors and brakes with heavy duty equipment, but had not upgraded the electronics. After a few years, the chair began to blow fuses. The belts had to be so tight that they would not disengage by simply pushing the levels on the sides, and so it was difficult to move the chair when it could not pull itself. I often repaired it where it broke down. Chet and I were attending church camp in Cisco, Texas, when the chair had a major breakdown. I was asleep in a cabin when a fellow ran in and shouted, "Chet's chair is on fire." I ran to the spot to see the chair going around in a tight circle and one motor smoking badly. Chet said that one motor would not respond to his control stick, and that it was running full speed forward. He locked the brake on the good motor and jumped out. I unplugged the motor from the power supply and stood back. It never did flame up, but was red hot. We replaced the motor while a replacement chair was being built. I felt that we had gotten as much out of that first chair as we could. We had friends in both Bossier and Bedford who were welders, and they had welded the red chair several times. The cushions showed wear, and I suppose we should have replaced the chair earlier.

Someone told me about Eddie Kelliher who ran a small wheelchair repair service out of his garage. He had been a Fort Worth policeman and was in a wheelchair himself. He just wanted to help folks who needed help with mobility. He built a new chair for Chet for only $2,000. It was lighter than his first chair, and it was not as fast. Still, it served him beautifully until he went to college. The chair that Mr. Kelliher built used the frame and seat from an Invacare Ranger II. He attached the foot rests together and made a step for Chet. Still, Chet found getting into the chair difficult. I built a second step into the front of the chair, and even wired the control box through a keyed switch which I buried into the wooden 2"X4" step. Chet's nephews quickly decided that this step made an excellent seat for them, individually. When he got the chair he now drives, the designer put a step in the same place as the one I built for the Ranger II and padded it. Niece Kayden joined the parade of nephews who love to ride Uncle Chet's chair.

We had heard that the state of Texas would help with expenses for the handicapped. However, when I called Texas Rehabilitation Commission, I was told that the help was extremely limited unless the handicapped person fit under a classification such as blind or deaf. When I asked why, I was told that those groups were large in number and had good lobbying support. I keep calling all over Texas until one person referred me to the Virginia Witt of the Fort Worth office of the Texas Rehabilitation Commission. She promised great support upon hearing about Chet. She said that there was a classification that Chet fit under perfectly. It was "Catastrophically Handicapped." That meant that Chet would get his college tuition paid by Texas. He would get help with a new chair and a van to carry it in. He would be taught to drive. Ms. Witt said that her job was to help Chet become a tax payer and pay her salary. Chet had to meet with Ms. Witt and make big promises. He had to have his report card sent to her during his last year in high school and in college. He had to make good grades and carry a full load of classes. She encouraged him to live on campus during his junior and senior years at the University of North Texas at Denton. Chet attended Tarrant County College during his first two years and lived at home. However, he was pleased to accept the advice of Ms. Witt and move to the next level of independent for his junior year.

Since Ms. Witt was experienced with mobility issues that Chet would face, she was of tremendous benefit in the giving advice. She first asked how old his chair was. Upon hearing that it was six years old, she got him a new one. She said that she did not want one of her students missing classes because of a broken down wheelchair. Ms. Witt was very pleased with Chet's attitude and grades. He attended Tarrant County College, a community junior college, for the first two years of his college work. The college was on the route that I took to my office and was less than two miles from my office. Therefore, I could drop Chet at TCC or pick him up quite easily. We often ate lunch together at the cafeteria on campus. Chet was soon involved and had friends at his new school. He found both high school and junior college easy. Since Chet had chosen the field of radio, television, and film, he soon got involved with the drama department on campus. To this day, he retains a great relationship with Stacy Schronk, the drama teacher. Chet preferred the back stage work, and Mr. Schronk taught him well in lighting, sound, and stage management. Even after Chet graduated from the University of North Texas, he has been privileged to work with Mr. Schronk in several productions in community theatre, working as stage manager and even as assistant director. Chet faced few, if any, accessibility issues at TCC. He refused to get involved with a handicap organization on campus because he did not want to be viewed as someone who constantly had issues with the school. Instead, he was known as one who worked around any issues he faced.

When Chet was nearing the finish of his work at TCC, the State of Texas agreed to furnish a van for him to drive. We were told to contact one of the State's providers, and we choose Advanced Mobility of Fort Worth. We bought a Plymouth Grand Voyager that met their specifications and waited. We waited for almost five months. Then, the word came to bring the van to Advanced Mobility because Texas Rehabilitation had made the funds available. I was amazed to learn that the adaptations on the van cost $60,000.00. When

we got the van back, TRC provided an Occupational Therapist who worked with Baylor Hospital to teach Chet his
driving skills. However, we did not wait on her. We used the
church parking lot to get started, and soon, we graduated to
the streets. One day, early in the process, I had Chet drive
the two of us to the Colleyville Elementary School where his
mother is the Assistant Principal. While he waited in the van,
I went inside and asked her to come outside for a surprise.
Since it was late in the day, there were few other cars around.
Judy had no idea of what I was up to, but grinned and com-
plied. Even after she saw the van, she did not know what we
had in mind until I opened the left side door and we both got
in the back. I called for Chet to drive us to the nearby junior
high school and back. She was a little nervous, but was extremely proud of him, too. Chet passed his driving test with
flying colors, and was even complimented by the state
trooper who gave him the driving test. Through a process of
several steps, the van can be converted to "able bodied
driver" mode. During the first few weeks Chet was enrolled
UNT, his roommate drove the van. Then, for the next several weeks, we wanted to make sure that someone was with
Chet while he was driving, in case he had any needs. His
roommate graciously rode with him. Then, the big day came
for Chet to drive from Bedford back to UNT in Denton by
himself alone. He looked forward to that Sunday afternoon,
and both his mother and I were nervous. When the time
came for him to leave, it was raining. We watched him drive
away, smiled at each other, and waited anxiously for his call
that said he was there having had no problems along the way.

Today, he drives all over Dallas and Fort Worth by himself.

Since Ms. Witt had encouraged Chet to move out of our house and live on campus during his last two college years, Chet chose the University of North Texas. UNT has a great department for radio, television, and film students. However, since Chet would need help dressing and eating, Ms Witt committed the state of Texas with its Rehabilitation Commission once again. Chet found that a friend from church wanted to go to UNT, and needed some financial assistance. Chet asked him to be his roommate, technically working for Chet, but paid by TRC. The first year went great for the two men, and they had a fine dorm room. Chet got involved with the Church of Christ Student Center just off campus, and soon he announced that he wanted to live there for his senior year. TRC did not mind that arrangement at all since the student center was cheaper than the dorm room. There was a student living there who was glad to be Chet's helper and get the financial assistance that TRC paid. At the student center, Chet led singing for the devotionals and even planned them. Soon, he and the campus minister, Eric Yates, became great friends. They are still very close today and Eric paid Chet several times to come and lead their weekend retreats. Chet chose to come home on most of the weekends, but he found that he needed to stay on campus sometimes. When he stayed at UNT on weekends, he attended the Singing Oaks Church of Christ. Soon, he preferred to stay there and go to church with Eric and his friends. He even led singing for the church a few Sundays.

To graduate with a B.A. in his chosen field, Chet had to do an internship at a radio station. He applied for and got the internship at KDGE, 102.1, and he felt that this was a major accomplishment. Most college interns did not get to be on air, but in his first week, the host of the morning show put a headset on him and interviewed live on air. It was a blast, according to Chet. During his days on campus, he worked both on air and as production engineer for the college radio station, KNTU. He was credited by the station manager as being one of their best engineers, and even after graduation he still went back to work the network production for some ballgames. He had a tall barstool prepared to make him high enough for his feet to reach the controls, and he would leave the barstool at the radio station at UNT. During the 2002 football season, the UNT team lost several games early. However, they lost no division games. Coincidently, Chet started doing the engineering at the time of the team's success. When the team was playing for the national championship, the radio announcer, an area professional, and the others associated with the school insisted that Chet be the engineer for the game. The team won the national championship, and the announcer said on air that they had not lost when Chet was the engineer. Judy does not like to listen to radio broadcasts of football games, but we were listening that night and heard that big announcement.

The day came for graduation from UNT. We gathered with a few friends and sat with a host of other proud parents in that large field house. The announcer even said "McDoniel" correctly, and then added, "Magna Cum Laude." The audience had applauded every graduate, but they stood and applauded Chet.

Chet has enjoyed using his degree in community theatre and in church work; however, he has not been able to find a job that directly utilizes his training. His education has been generally beneficial to him in his business. Chet worked for a travel agency for 5 years, and now owns "Off to Neverland Travel" which is a full-service travel agency that specializes in Disney vacations. He does most of his work online, and is able to work out of the house with this job. He has also developed "42 Productions," a video production and web hosting and design company. He makes videos for weddings and any other occasions of remembrance. He also develops and hosts websites for several businesses. He also has developed a speaking business, and he and I have gotten to present our story locally and in several different places all around the country. He often sings for weddings, funerals, and other special occasions. His college work is beneficial in all these efforts to serve and to earn a living. Chet believes a man should be happy in his work, but that if he can not find the job he wants, he must find another way to make a living!

Chet Says: I do appreciate all of the ways I was served by living in Texas. Particularly, Texas Rehabilitation Commission (now known as Division for Rehabilitation Services), has been an immense help, and I did not mind one bit having to show my grades to my TRC counselor. Especially since she told me that I had the highest grades of any of her clients.

College was where I truly learned about myself and how I could live "on my own" away from my parents. I really enjoyed my time at the Christian Campus Center, and have just as many crazy stories as I do for my high school years. At the CCC, I served as an intern not only for the worship devotionals, but also as a "listener" for other students. There were two other guys that lived at the CCC, and we were "on call" twenty-four hours a day. From picking up someone who had a flat at 3AM to talking into the wee hours of the night to someone struggling with their faith, I was always ready to help.

I will never forget September 11, 2001. It was on that horrible day when I truly learned how big the family of the Lord truly is. I awoke to the sound of Eric Yates (the Campus Minister) pounding on my door telling me to get up because we were already flooded with students walking in off the street wanting to pray with us. Classes were cancelled, of course, and I along with many other group members spent the entire day in prayer. I cried with some students who did not know the whereabouts of their family members, and laughed in joy with others when their phones finally rang with familiar voices on the other end ensuring the safety of their loved ones. I would have never been able to serve on that day or any other in such a capacity had a stayed at home. I learned much more in my relationships with others while living away from home than I could have ever learned in the classroom. But, don't tell the state of Texas...they paid quite a bit for my education.

I wouldn't trade my time away from home for anything, but I did enjoy returning home on many weekends.

8

JONI

In 1995, the Sneed family came to the Pipeline Road Church of Christ, and they had a seventh grade daughter named, Joni, who rather quickly caught Chet's attention. Before long they were "going together." The relationship continued for months, but like most romances of that age group, they eventually went their separate ways. During some of their high school years, they were not close, even to the point of not speaking to each other, but when they got to their college years, they became friends again.

We often hosted the College Age Life Group that met on the second Sunday evening of each month. We would have a devotional and discussion, and then, Judy and I would feed the group. We noticed that Chet often sat with Joni, especially at eating time, and she helped him with his food. She seemed to accept this chore with ease, and they could get quite involved in conversation while eating.

Eventually, Mandy joined the group and immediately became fast friends of both Chet and Joni. During college breaks, the three went several places together and spent hours together at Mandy's apartment and sometimes at our house. After Chet graduated from UNT, the threesome seemed to be together more. When Joni graduated from Oklahoma Christian University, the three began to call themselves "The Three Amigos." They loved the humor of the movie by that same name and still quote lines from it.

In May, 2004, Chet and I went to Disney World for "Free-Wheelin' Disney 2005." The company he worked for suggested that he lead a group of mobility impaired people on a trip to the Walt Disney World® Resort and on a cruise onboard the Disney Wonder®. He needed to go to Florida early to work on his "Universal Specialist" certification, and so, we were gone for nine days. The trip was great, but I began to miss my wife. One night, I told him how much I missed her, and he added, "I am anxious to get home to my friends, too." Since he and Joni emailed each other everyday while we were on that trip, I asked him if he missed Joni specifically, and he answered with a firm "Yes." We had only been home from that trip a month when Chet told Joni how much he missed her, and that he wanted more than just a friend in her. She responded just the way he had hoped, and their romance blossomed rapidly.

Judy and I had promised ourselves not to try to live the future before it comes, but we had tried to look into the future some. We believed that someday Chet would marry. We talked about how that time would probably come in his late twenties or thirties. We thought that most teenagers and even most college students are so caught up with physical appearance that a pretty girl would be reluctant to develop a relationship with a man without arms and with short legs. We knew that when he and his friends got a little older, some would look past the limb deficiency and see a great person in that body. I remember teaching a class at the Pipeline Church of Christ when the subject of Chet and his future came into the discussion. The large class offered several warm comments about how our family had adapted well to the challenges of Chet's handicap. Some added that he would have a fine life. For some reason that I do not remember now, I added, "Yes, he is doing well, and someday he is going to marry one of your daughters." The class got rather quiet. Then, someone asked, "Why not?"

In August, 2004, Chet gave Joni an engagement ring, and they began to plan a May, 2005, wedding. Joni had just agreed to begin work with a day care center. While she was pleased to get work, this was not what she wanted. Her degree is in elementary education, and she had wanted to be a classroom teacher. Before she could begin her job, Judy suddenly had an opening at her school for a special education assistant. Joni was hired, and began that strange relationship of working under the assistant principal who was the mother of her boyfriend and soon to become her fiancé. However, this new job made a May wedding date untenable. They moved the date the direction we expected—earlier. Chet and Joni were married at the spring break, March 19, 2005.

We wholeheartedly approved of Chet's choice of Joni to be his wife, but we had very little say in the matter. We taught our children to make their own decisions, and I do not plan to go through life making  decisions for them. I feel that I have all I can handle just working on me. Still, I wondered how secure Chet and Joni were in their relationship as they approached marriage. I wished that I could watch them in public when they were not aware of my presence. I got my wish in November, 2004. Chet chose to go to a "Seminar at Sea" on a cruise ship. I thought it was a good idea since he had never sailed with the cruise line that invited the travel agents to this seminar. Judy and I had committed to go with him on the trip when he first booked it in the early part of summer, 2004. After Chet asked Joni to marry him, he decided to take her on the trip, too. Now, that meant that four of us would be together in the small room on the ship, and we would get to observe their interaction from a rather close vantage point. More importantly, we would see them on the ship when they did not see us. Often, Judy and I went our way, and Joni and Chet went a different direction. Several times, we saw them when they did not see us. I was delighted to see Joni being attentive to Chet and showing by her actions that she was glad to be with him. Occasionally, Judy and I would find ourselves in conversation with strangers on the ship, and mention that we were with our travel agent son, Chet and his fiancé. As soon as Chet and Joni were identified, the people conversing with us would volunteer, "She is so attentive to him." I told her about those conversations, and I told her that I thank God for her.

Joni wrote her relatives to tell them about Chet. Her mother gave us a copy of the letter, and Joni, reluctantly, allowed me to include a portion of her letter here.

"Chet comes from a wonderful family. His dad is the preacher at the Legacy Church of Christ where we both grew up. His mom is the assistant principal at the school where I am working now. He has an older brother and sister who are both married. He has three nephews and two nieces. They are all really sweet! Chet graduated from the University of North Texas in 2002 with a degree in Radio, Television and Film Production. He is now working as a travel agent. Chet also has his own company that creates slideshows out of pictures and puts them on a DVD. He has done a lot of those for weddings and some for anniversaries.

Chet is able to do all these things and so much more despite his special needs. He was born with a limb deficiency. Many of the things that we do with our hands, he is able to do with his feet. He uses a wheelchair and has a van that is adapted for him to drive. Chet doesn't let anything get in the way of what he wants to do. He has been able to travel a lot (mostly to Disney World). Last May, he led a group of people in wheelchairs through Disney World on a trip called Free-Wheelin' Disney. He already has another scheduled for next year.

Chet has an incredible spirit and love for God. It is evident in the way he lives his life, and I know he will be an incredible spiritual leader for us and our future family. I have never seen Chet as someone who was different. I have always loved him, first as a friend and now as my future husband. We both understand that our marriage will be more difficult than most, but I know I feel that it would be even more difficult for us to not be together. Please keep us in your thoughts and prayers as we begin this part of our lives."

Joni's parents struggled with the thought of her marrying

Chet. One Sunday morning, Judy and Joni's mother spent an hour talking about him and what he could do. That conversation really helped Lisa. After the Sneeds put aside their reservations about the marriage, Lisa told Judy that Joni had convinced her that she was sure she wanted to marry Chet; and since Joni was sure, they would be supportive of her plans. I had a good visit with Frank, Joni's father, and the four of us worked well together as parents to plan for a beautiful beginning to their marriage.

Chet Says: I could write an entire book about my incredible wife. She is amazing. From the moment we started dating (the 2nd time…after college), I knew she was the one. She took all my fears and easily pushed them away, and today we share not only a beautiful marriage, but a beautiful friendship. In just a few chapters, I'll explain why I believe her to be the most amazing woman ever!

9

"I DO"

March 19, 2005, finally arrived. Chet told me that when they were first engaged, March 19 was over 200 days away, and that seemed like an eternity. When the "countdown" on the computer dropped below 200, that was significant, but when it dropped to a double digit number of days, that was better. Then, when they were within 30 days of the wedding, they were able to go buy the license, and their plan seemed even more real. Finally, the day came and all was ready. I felt that Chet and Joni did an excellent job of preparing for their wedding, and an even better job of preparing for marriage. They seldom, if ever, seemed stressed about their wedding plans. Occasionally, their families made them feel some stress over the preparation.

Joni and Chet felt that their wedding should be uniquely theirs, but I wish that some of the plans that made their different would become standard for all weddings. For example, they rejected all the "luck" aspects of the wedding. They claim that a couple must choose between luck and God. They chose to see one another, in wedding attire, before the actual wedding. They got dressed early and met in the worship center at 12:45. Chet arrived first and took his seat where he would sit during the ceremony. We pulled screens in front of the doors so no one could see inside the worship center. Joni entered to greet her groom, and they spent twenty minutes together in private. Chet later told me that those twenty minutes were priceless. That time together removed all nervousness from the actual moment of the wedding and allowed the two of them to be much more composed. Chet and Joni talked about their plans and the moment, and prayed. Then, after those twenty private minutes, all pictures were taken. All family members were to be there early, and all the wedding party pictures were taken, too. Nothing was left to delay the reception after the wedding.

I performed all three of my children's weddings, and all three chose to face the audience with me standing with my back to the audience. Since standing for the duration of the wedding would have been difficult for Chet, he and Joni chose to sit in straight chairs facing the audience. Then, the audience could see their faces and see the exchange of rings.

Chet and I, with his four groomsmen close behind us, stood facing the audience as the bride's maids came down the isle. The audience probably wondered why we were smiling so big when one of the bride's maids stuck her tongue out at Chet and grinned. Just before Joni's song started, I asked the audience to remain seated while she entered so that Chet could see her from his lower vantage point. After Frank gave Joni away, Chet stepped down a couple of the stairs to meet her. I stepped to the side until they were seated. I thanked the audience on behalf of Chet and Joni and then, announced that Joni's great uncle, Harold Sneed, would lead us in prayer. Then, I took my position and began to address Chet and Joni. They paid total attention.

During the rehearsal, Chet told me what to say at the point of exchanging rings. I simply said, "Chet, give Joni the ring you have brought for her and repeat after me." Later, "Joni, give Chet the ring you have brought for him and repeat after me." Thus, there were no awkward words about putting the ring on his toe, which she did. Both Chet and Joni spoke boldly, but for the vows, all they wanted to say was "I do." I characteristically give couples the option of repeating nearly all the words after me, writing their own vows, or just answering "I do."

The two of them planned a simple, elegant wedding. They were concerned that the focus be on getting married, not on a show. Chet sang, but his song, "I Will Be Here," was prerecorded, and the CD was played at the wedding. Chet wanted his focus on Joni and the wedding, not on a singing performance. Joni entered to "Still in Love," and their recessional was "Wrapped Up in You." Near the end of the recessional, just as the last grandparents were nearing the rear of the auditorium, the music dropped in volume, and Chet's recorded voice came on, saying, "Thank you for joining us for our celebration. A reception has been prepared at the end of the Grand Concourse. If you would like to attend, please exit the auditorium, take a right, and head down to the end of the hall. Joni and I have already taken all of our pictures and await seeing you at the reception. Thanks, and God bless!" The volume came back up just in time for the audience to hear a final, "wrapped up in you." The timing of all the music was perfect thanks to Chet's class called Digital Music Editing. The processional song ended a couple of seconds after Frank and Joni arrived at the front and Chet moved to

meet her. The recessional song ended just as the grandparents got to the back.

Since the wedding was at 3PM, we only served

light refreshments at the reception. However, the groom's table was unique. His cake was in the shape of Mickey Mouse. Everyone knew that both of them are huge Disney fans, and their honeymoon was at Disney World. We served Dr. Pepper at the groom's table, and that is the drink Chet and Joni drank together at the reception.

Lisa's employer had a refurbished Model T. She arranged for him to carry the couple away in the Model T. The car itself drew considerable attention. Again, resisting any appeal to luck, nothing was thrown at the couple as they made their way to the Model T. They drove to the Sneed's, only a minute from the building, where the two of them changed clothes, and I picked them up in fifteen minutes. I had already moved Chet's chair to his van, and I dropped them off at the van. They took off to the DFW Airport Hyatt, and I picked up the van the next day. Chet had called to tell me where it was in the airport parking.

The entire wedding was bright and happy. Joni and Chet, far from crying as some brides and grooms do, smiled most of time. Judy and I received some comments about how broad our smiles were. More people stayed for this reception than I have ever seen stay. Of course, taking all pictures before the ceremony was a major contributor to their staying, but the joy of the occasion contributed, too.

All relatives, who were able, came to be a part of the grand occasion and to support us. We deeply appreciate everyone who came, but especially two families. All aunts, uncles, and even cousins in Chet's family are considerably older than he is, except for Jane and J.P., Pat's children. Since we spent a lot of time with the McCarleys while I was preaching in Kentucky and since we spent so many Christmases together, Chet was closer to Jane and J.P. than any other family members. Jane and Jeff and J.P. and Autumn, with their children, flew in on Friday evening and came to our house as soon as they could. I had performed the weddings of Jane and J.P., and at all of these family wedding, we have had the custom of singing together some time during the festivities. We were all looking forward to a time of family singing at this wedding.

The rehearsal and dinner lasted until 9PM, but then, Chet, Joni, the groomsmen, and a host of our relatives gathered after that at our house and sang until Judy called a halt at about 1AM. Joni, Chet and the groomsman left before the singing was done, but I doubt they got any more sleep than we did. We gathered again on Saturday evening (after the wedding), but Chet and Joni, somehow, did not choose to join us this time. When we offered to let them join us, Chet boldly declared, "No way."

March 19, 2005, was a grand time. The wedding was perfect. The huge crowd of friends and relatives at the wedding and the reception were a genuine delight. The happiness of Joni and Chet was so obvious. The day lives brightly in my memory.

Everything would be different after March 19. Judy and I are enjoying our empty nest. Chet and I still eat lunch together, and I hear about how wonderful everything is in his world. They used to live in an apartment only a few minutes from us, but now they own a house about 30 minutes away. Joni was particularly pleased after a recent meeting she was a part of because he got to introduce herself as "Joni McDoniel." Chet speaks of the joy of not having to go to separate homes at the end of the day, and of waking up next to one another.

Yet, not everything is totally different. In the wedding message, I said to Chet, "Chet you have always lived your life to glory of God. One of your themes has been to focus on what you have, not on what you don't have, and use it to the glory of God. Hold on to that concept, and now, use your marriage to the glory of God."

Chet Says: We had a blast at our wedding, and we took pride in making it our own. So much of a traditional wedding ceremony is based on pagan traditions and secular beliefs. I've always said that I don't need luck, I've got the Lord. Luck is a secular belief that is generally associated with earthly riches and fortune. Since God created the Earth, and He's on my side, it seems to me that I don't need luck. The time Joni and I shared together before the ceremony was more precious than the ceremony itself. I highly recommend trashing the "bad luck" garbage and try actually spending some quiet time with your soon-to-be spouse on your wedding day.

Beyond all of the ceremony, I appreciate that our parents recognized that we planned for a marriage more than a ceremony. Many classes, many books, and most importantly, tons of time spent talking about what we wanted in life all helped prepare us. We knew then like we know now that we are on the same path together in life. We have the same goals and dreams which makes our marriage very strong. I value the time we spent preparing for a marriage as it has greatly helped us in our union. The wedding was fun, too, but it only lasted a few moments…the marriage lasts a lifetime.

10

IT'S NOT A SIN
TO BE IN THE PITS

During some of the early days of Chet's life, Judy cried her-self to sleep every night. Even today, she has struggled with having input in this writing. Most, if not all parents of handicapped children, know the pain and despair that we feel. There is a danger in presenting the bright, happy successes of Chet's life. Someone reading this book for encouragement could feel discouragement. Living with the fact that we brought a handicapped child into the world is difficult. His bright outlook on life and his success in several endeavors can not change the fact that we still feel pain. Generally, we choose not to talk about that pain. Talking about it at this point only causes us feel the pain afresh. Yet, the reality of that pain is a vital part of our message.

One of Satan's meanest tricks is to cause people to feel bad because they are feeling bad. Many of us were taught that we should not let life's troubles get us down. So, when we are feeling down, we are failing, and we feel worse. Some have even thought that if we have faith, we will never know depression. That is not true. It is part of Satan's lie. It is not a sin to be in the pits.

The very word "depression" is used in different ways today. Everybody has the "Monday blues" once in a while. Monday blues become a problem when they last until Friday. Churchill referred to depression as the "black dog." Lucy Freeman has called it the "silent scream." Sometimes, we use the word loosely to mean feeling slightly down, but that probably is a misuse of the word. Clinical depression is a feeling of gloom, hopelessness, loneliness, self-pity, anger, and being trapped. Clinical depression can not be helped with pep talks or quick remedies. "Whistling in the dark," "forcing a smile," or "picking up you chin" may help with Monday blues, but we only do damage when we suggest those remedies for true depression. Thank God for antidepressants and the physicians who know how to administer them. Still, realizing that we are not offending God or failing ourselves when we are depressed is important to being able to receive help for any depression, including clinical depression.

Some of God's greatest servants faced times when they we "down." Consider David's words in Psalms 31:9-13. He says:

"Be merciful to me, O LORD, for I am in distress;
my eyes grow weak with sorrow,
my soul and my body with grief.
My life is consumed by anguish
and my years by groaning;
my strength fails because of my affliction,
and my bones grow weak.
Because of all my enemies,
I am the utter contempt of my neighbors;
I am a dread to my friends—
those who see me on the street flee from me.
I am forgotten by them as though I were dead;
I have become like broken pottery.
For I hear the slander of many;
there is terror on every side;
they conspire against me
and plot to take my life."

David was describing a feeling that many have suffered, and yet, it was not clinical depression. David was able to lay aside the feelings he expressed by turning back (verse 14) to say, "But I trust in you, O Lord."

Jeremiah had so much sorrow that he is known as "the weeping prophet." Consider his words of Jeremiah 20:14-15:

> "Cursed be the day I was born!
> May the day my mother bore me not be blessed!
> Cursed be the man who brought my father the news,
> who made him very glad, saying,
> 'A child is born to you—a son!'"

Many people will identify with Job's feeling expressed in his 7th chapter. He writes:

> "so I have been allotted months of futility,
> and nights of misery have been assigned to me.
> When I lie down I think, 'How long before I get up?'
> The night drags on, and I toss till dawn." (Job 7:3-4)

Elijah's story may the one that offers the greatest hope. His depression is clear, and he was not condemned by God for it. Elijah won a tremendous victory on Mount Carmel. Most of the nation of Israel had left the worship of God and followed Queen Jezebel in her worship of Baal and Asherah (the female counterpart of Baal). (I Kings 18) Elijah called for the nation to assemble at Mount Carmel. He challenged the 450 prophets of Baal and the 400 prophets of Asherah. He called for them to cut up a bull for sacrifice to their god, put it on an altar, and call for their god to send fire to consume it. He would prepare a sacrifice and call for Jehovah to send fire to consume it. The prophets of Baal pleaded with their stone god to send fire to consume their offering. That hunk of stone did nothing. Elijah prepared his offering and soaked it with water to help the people know there was no trickery involved. He prayed to God, and God sent fire that consumed the offering, the altar, and the water around the altar. The people announced, "Jehovah is God." They killed all the prophets of the false gods that day. Then, Elijah asked God to send rain to end the three year drought that God had sent because the people were idolatrous. God sent the rain, and everybody went home happy.

Not everybody was happy. Jezebel sent word to Elijah, "May the gods deal with me, be it ever so severely, if by this time tomorrow I do not make your life like that of one of them." By "them" she meant her dead prophets. Upon receiving her threat, that brave prophet who had stood against 850 false prophets before a nation in assembly, turned and ran. He ran from Jezreel in the middle of Israel to Mount Horeb in the Sinai Peninsula. There he hid in a cave. God helped him on his journey and let him have his "down time" for thirty days. When God eventually asked Elijah what he was doing hiding in the cave, Elijah expressed his frustration and despair. He said, "I have been very zealous for the LORD God Almighty. The Israelites have rejected your covenant, broken down your altars, and put your prophets to death with the sword. I am the only one left, and now they are trying to kill me too." (I Kings 19:10) God did not say, "Shame on you." He did begin to correct Elijah's thinking and his attitude. God showed Elijah His power. He told him that he was wrong about being the only one who stood for God. Seven thousand had not "bowed the knee to Baal." Then, God gave Elijah some work to do. He said, "Go back the way you came, and go to the Desert of Damascus. When you get there, anoint Hazael king over Aram. Also, anoint Jehu son of Nimshi king over Israel, and anoint Elisha son of Shaphat from Abel Meholah to succeed you as prophet." (I Kings 19:15-16)

Elijah was not where God wanted him to be, and God corrected him. Still, God did not shame him or condemn him. This is the same Elijah who was taken to heaven without having to die, and only two men have had that privilege. Evidently, God wanted the world to know what He thinks of a man who will stand like Elijah stood. I find encouragement in the fact that this great man suffered depression, at least, at this one point. While Elijah did not sin by being down, he could not accomplish God's work until he got out of the cave and out of the blues.

Judy and I have tried to follow God's prescription for Elijah. We have allowed ourselves some down time, more than once. We have gone back to the Bible to see God's power and love. We have adjusted our view of our situation and life's purposes. We have gone to work to serve others.

Much of our grieving has been private. We did not want to present a picture of despair to Chet. We did all we could to teach him to have an optimistic view of life. We did not want to discourage anyone watching us. But most of all, the pain was ours, and it was private.

I learned from our own situation to deal patiently with others who are depressed. I try to assure them that God is not angry with them for being down. It is not a sin to be in the pits, but its no way to live either. Elijah needed some down time, but eventually, he had to get out of the cave. Judy and I still hurt, but we refuse to live in a cave. By God's patience, mercy, and strength, we climbed out of the pit.

Chet Says: I'm so glad that we have a biblical model for depression and God's view of it. I have feared, before, that in our presentations, we come across as "too optimistic." How could that be? There are people in the world who are hurting from depression, and we have to be careful not to condemn their depression through our optimism. We do all we can to help people out of that pit, but we show love and compassion while helping. Christians have been some of the worst at offering advice. We should be, and I am, thankful for medicines, doctors and therapists that help those who are suffering. Our God is love, and He hurts for those who suffer. We should mirror that love in our relationships and understand that depression is real, and that our support to our loved ones is some of the best medicine available!

11

ATTITUDE IS
WHAT'S IMPORTANT

Long before Chet was born, Judy and I believed that a healthy attitude is vital to a child's development. We tried hard to teach a good outlook on life to Randy and Jennifer. When we began training Chet, we felt even more strongly that teaching him the right attitudes and views of himself was essential. There is one thing worse than having a handicapped child, and that is having a handicapped child with a bad attitude. I have told my family that several times. The specific bad attitude that I have seen is the whiney, poor me, mad at the world, the world owes me, or generally a chip on the shoulder because I was born with a problem. It is neither a correct view of life nor a profitable way to live.

I have tried in some of the preceding chapters to tell some of the basic views we tried to give Chet. Believing that the greatest model we can present to other families is to be found in this arena, I have chosen to be as specific as I can be in naming the lesson of life we tried to impart to Chet.

Nobody Owes You

Soon after Chet was born, Judy and I heard about a group of parents who had handicapped children. They met regularly to support one another and talk about the problem they faced. We were looking for any help we could find, and so we quickly joined them. However, we did not stay with the group long because we did not like the attitudes we heard expressed. The basic view that troubled us was that others owed us something because of our children. I felt that several of them wanted pity. More specifically, they had a host of complaints against the education system in Louisiana, both public and private. They complained that the teachers and administrators did not want their children, would not talk fairly to them, and forthrightly violated the laws of the state designed to assure education to the handicapped. Their basic position was adversarial, and we struggled with that position. I think Judy saw the problems with their thinking first because she is a teacher. She taught five years before she stopped to rear our children. Also, she substituted in Apollo Elementary during the time that Randy and Jennie were there. She had a great relationship with the teachers, administrators, and even the school board members that she knew. She was confident that the members of this group could not be viewing the schools correctly. Further, we just believe in something more positive.

I don't know that we ever tried to tell Chet about that early experience with the parents' group, but I trust that it did reinforce our determination not to present a "poor me" attitude to any of our children. Randy and Jennie took Chet with them on many of their outings. I even built a soft seat for him between the two bucket seats of that Ford Courier pickup they drove everywhere. (I now know that the seat belt was good only for stopping and cornering and would have been of little benefit in an accident. I am glad to report it was never tested.) They proudly showed off Chet's latest tricks and bits of cuteness to their friends.

Judy and I never tried to hide our lives. What would have been abnormal to others was normal for us. This is who our family was, and we were proud of all of the members. We boldly took Chet with us to Sea World, Disney World, on a Disney Cruise, Six Flags over Texas, Six Flags over Georgia, to the beach in Alabama, to concerts, and family gatherings.

Chris Webster used to take Chet to concerts, especially country music concerts. She generally got to take him backstage, and we have pictures of him with Reba McIntire, Marty Stuart, Glen Campbell, and some performers I don't know. I could not control Chris, but she knew this made me uncomfortable. I feared too much privilege could cause Chet to think he was entitled to special advantages because he is handicapped. I am pleased to report that he only learned to enjoy country music. One of their trips nearly turned disastrous. Chris took him to hear Hank Williams, Jr. She stood in life for a day and got front row seats. However, when Hank started singing, the crowd blindly rushed the stage and were about to crush Chet. Their friend Dan was nearby and saw their problem. Dan stands over six feet tall and had muscles like Sylvester Stallone. He grabbed Chet and fought his way through the wild crowd. Poor Chris was scared badly, but they were ready to go again, to a calmer concert.

When Chet was in high school, I had to go help him one day because his chair was dead. When it rained, moisture could get into the control box on the chair, and it would immediately become a heavy push chair. While I was pushing him to class in the rain, we found a maintenance truck blocking the wide sidewalk. The workers nearby made no effort to move the truck. I had to push the chair off the sidewalk and into soft ground. I struggled, but managed to push it through the mud, and we went on our way. Before returning to my office, I paid a visit to the office of an assistant principal of the large high school. As gently as I could, I complained. I wanted to show sympathy for the workers who wanted to get as close as possible to their work site, but I thought their convenience was put ahead of the students, especially anyone in a wheelchair. The assistant principal grew angry at the maintenance workers and promised that the problem would be solved when Chet came out of the classroom. A quick solution would be important since another student was to push him to his next class. When I saw the administrators' strong reaction, I explained, "We don't feel like anyone owes us anything." He quickly answered, "Oh yes they do! They owe courtesy and consideration. I expect us to open doors and move any obstacles in Chet's way." Chet reported that the truck had been moved when he came out of the classroom. I realize that we all owe one another courtesy and consideration. As a society, we must build sidewalk cutouts, automatic openers on doors in public buildings, and even provide elevators. Still, I was concerned that Chet not feel that the maintenance workers owed him special consideration.

When Chet was in the local junior college, Tarrant County College, he was asked to join a group of handicapped students. He wasn't interested. He told me that he did not want to be a part of a group of complainers who always had something against the university. I was extremely pleased to hear him announce that he did not like the whiny attitude of the group. One of the members of the group was a bright personality. Several times, I saw her call to Chet to wait for her. Her chair was a non-powered chair. She would hold to the handle on Chet's powered chair, and shout, "Let's go, Chet."

Even she, with her fun loving approach, could not persuade Chet to go to the handicapped students meetings. At times, I am not sure he knew he was handicapped.

Never Be Afraid To Try

When I was in the eleventh grade in Tuckerman High School in Arkansas, my dad taught me a lesson that I chose to pass on to our children. I told Dad that I had considering becoming a candidate for the presidency of the student council for my senior year, but that I was scared to run. He asked me what I was afraid of, and I quickly answered, "Loosing the election." He replied, "What's so bad about loosing? You can't win unless you run." I lost, but I came within three votes of the winner. Also, my losing that election did not hurt me in any way. Judy supported me as I pressed this lesson on Randy and Jennie.

When Chet turned sixteen, he was pleased that he could get a job. I suppose both Judy and I wondered who would hire a boy without arms. Several of Chet's friends went to a job fair at Six Flags Over Texas and were hired there. Chet asked me to take him. Judy says today that she thought that I was cruel when I took him to Six Flags. She saw his excitement and feared a major disappointment. She even tried to warn both of us, but he was determined. Six Flags was glad to have him apply. He was hired on the spot and told when to report for training. When we came home, he hurried into the house, slung his large envelope of training material across the floor, and announced, "Meet the newest hire of Six Flags." His time at Six Flags was extremely valuable to him, and they treated him very nicely. Chet worked at a simulated ride called "The Right Stuff" his first year. The supervisors saw his attitude, willingness to work, and his physical ability, and moved him into the role of shift supervisor on a roller coaster called "Flashback" during his second year. He actually operated Flashback from a control booth. He could not have had those opportunities if he had not been willing to try.

Accept a Challenge

Chet always did well academically, even in college. He seldom took notes, and still made "A's." One teacher at Tarrant County College tried to make her students prepare harder for her tests by telling them that no one did well on her tests. She told them that no student had ever made a "100%" on her test. Chet said within himself, "I will." The next day, the teacher saw Chet on the elevator, and asked, "Well, Chet, are you ready for my test?" He responded, "I was born ready." She continued, "So you think you will do well on it, do you?" He boldly announced, "I will make a 100, and He did. When she handed back the papers, she said, "Chet made a 100, and no one has ever done that before." He boldly added, "I told you I would." After that day, he and that teacher seemed to like one another.

In the rest of his college work, Chet was not afraid of any subject or test. In his work "on air" at the radio station on the campus of the University of North Texas, Chet sounded confident. When he worked as the engineer on KNTU, he showed such confidence that the professional announcer loved to hear that he was running the show. He accepts challenges well still today.

Use What You Have to Serve Jesus

I covered, in chapter six, an important lesson we tried to pass on to Chet. Some people spend their days wishing their lives or bodies were different. I believe we should spend our days using what we have to serve the Lord. The focus must be on what we have, not on what we don't have. Everyone is handicapped in some way. All of us have thought about what we could do if only we had something that we do not have.

Chet does not have arms, but he has a marvelous singing voice. He does not have fingers, but he can use toes. He does not have a whole body, but he has a brilliant mind. We tried to teach Chet to use what he has. We taught our other children the same lesson. In their cases, the lesson may not have been as dramatic, but it was equally important.

I have even seen some people reverse a problem and turn it into a tool of service. I have known of widows who use their painful experience to help other widows. Most victim groups were started by someone who was mistreated, and then, decided to help others who were similarly mistreated. I suppose that those who have suffered would rather not have had the experience that qualifies them to help others, but they did. Now, what will they do with that reality? We can sit and whine about our misfortune, or we can live for the Lord. I don't believe we can do both at the same time.

I have seen churches sing especially enthusiastically and thoughtfully when Chet leads singing. He knows music, has a great voice, has good stage presence, and these gifts make him an excellent song leader. However, the mere fact that he is handicapped can move people closer to the Lord when he leads worship. One lady told me that Chet's leading moved her in exactly that way. She was visiting at Legacy one day when Chet lead singing. She did not know that I am his father. She approached me because I was the preacher. She told me that she had come to church feeling "down" and hardly wanting to be there at all. She added, "But when I saw that man leading singing and looking so excited when he did not have arms, I wanted to sing."

Early in Chet's attendance at the Richland Hills Church of Christ, he had a powerful impact on a lady who writes a weekly email to a Bible class which she serves as secretary. The church was standing while singing the song, "The Joy of the Lord." Evonne Coleman gave me permission to include a portion of her email regarding what happened as the church was singing. She writes,

> "Out of my peripheral vision, I noticed that the gentleman in front of me was not standing. This did not

stop me from singing; but inspired me to just sing louder.

'The joy of the Lord will be my strength;
I will not falter, I will not faint.
He is my Shepherd I am not afraid;
The joy of the Lord is my strength.'
Even above my singing, now, I could hear him joining in....

'The joy of the Lord,
The joy of the Lord,
The joy of the Lord is my strength.'

As we began the second verse I was a little disappointed that he was not joining us in showing his joy by clapping.   I came to the part, again, where we were to begin clapping I glanced to see if I had inspired him to join us. This man had no hands! He didn't even have any arms. I was so shocked at my pride that I fell into my seat....on my pew.

However at this level (at his level), I could hear (and see) with much more understanding. This young man was singing from the heart about a JOY he knew first hand, from the Lord. I staggered to my feet, and began to try to sing, again. Only now I could hear what he was singing...

'The joy of the Lord will by my strength.
He will up-hold me all of my days.
I am surrounded by mercy and grace;
The joy of the Lord is my strength.'

And from this vantage point I could now see REAL JOY. He was clapping with his bare feet!"

The point is, use what you have rather than spending your time and thought on what you don't have. I love the way Chet has accepted this lesson and put it into practice.

Don't Sit on the Sidelines

When Judy and I attended college classes, we sat near the front. When we are in training groups, and the leader calls for volunteers to try the skill, we volunteer. We believe that you learn more that way and have more fun.

We tried to pass this "life-lesson" on to all three of our children, and all three seem to have accepted it. All three were regarded as leaders in whatever group they found themselves. Chet was never the quiet one in the group. He was often elected to a position or office in a group because he was willing to think and to say what he was thinking. I led a college age life group at our house for six years, and we often said that Chet and I led it together. He led the singing, but also, he was vital to any discussion of the lessons I presented. Chet and I like the words of Lee Ann Womack's "I Hope

You Dance." I understand that some of the lines from her song have become scrapbook titles. The thought I have tried to tell my children is expressed well in Womack's line: "And when you get the chance to sit it out or dance, I hope you dance." Chet seldom if ever has chosen "to sit it out."

Be a Christian

The most important lesson we tried to teach was "be a Christian." Being a Christian is not just a matter of having your name on a church role or attending worship assemblies. Those are important, but we tried to teach all three kids to live their lives in service to God. I believe that real Christianity finds its essence in service.

At one point in his teen years, Chet told me that he was feeling a bit overwhelmed because so many of his friends told him their troubles. He told me, "I am not a counselor." I advised him to be a good listener. I tried to take some pressure off of him by explaining that he did not have to have all the answers to his friends' problems, but he could serve them by listening.

I do not believe that we should do what everyone around us thinks we should do or wants us to do. Each has to determine his own talents and interests, and then, use those talents in the way he chooses.

Chet has found a host of ways to use his talents to the glory of God. I have already spoken about his song leading. He, also, had a singing group, Hessed. They put on fantastic concerts, and released two CDs (which can be purchased online at chetmcdoniel.com). He has taught classes at church. He and I have presented countless lessons jointly at various assemblies. He planned devotionals for the Christian Campus Center on the campus of UNT. He often does "voice-overs" for announcements at the Richland Hills Church of Christ. When he was in early high school, he helped me get started doing a daily devotional on line. While in high school, he taught me how to develop PowerPoint slides and convinced me that I should use them in my sermons. When he was in late high school, he took a brief course in HTML, and then, designed the first website for the Pipeline Road Church of Christ. Today, he has developed that skill to the point that he designs website professionally. In addition to these public services, Chet has been a friend to many who did not feel accepted in the group. Chet serves the Lord!

I trust that they are several other lessons that we taught. I believe these six shaped Chet. Chet gets much credit for where he is in life. Parents can teach important lessons to their children, but the children themselves must accept the lessons and make specific applications to their lives. I admire my son for what he has done with his life. In the face of severe physical limits, Chet thinks of possibilities.

12

CHET'S SAY

Reading this book has brought back many memories. I do remember some bad times, but most of my memories are good. No...great! I am a very positive person. That is due in large part to my upbringing as you have seen in the previous chapters; however, there is one main reason that I have this outlook. Want the answer? Want the secret of living a happy life no matter what your circumstance? Simple. The Lord sent His only son to die for my sins so that I can live with Him for all eternity. If that doesn't make you happy and give you a positive outlook on live, nothing will.

Satan is the all-time best discourager this world has ever seen. I would be lying if I told you I've never been discouraged. There have been times in my life when I really felt no reason to keep on going. Those are the times when I relied on my parents, my friends, and most importantly, my God. I would guess that every person on this Earth has, at one time or another, lost the will to keep fighting on through daily life. Satan is good at his self-given job. Some have asked me if I have ever questioned God. I have had my weak times, and yes, I've gotten mad at God regarding my condition. You know what I finally realized? God is big enough to take my anger, and just as you would a confused child, He put His arms around me in the midst of my tantrum and comforted me until the storm has passed. I must add that most of my questioning came in junior high. I no longer feel the need to question because I have come to know a better way to live. That is, serve God no matter what you have or don't have because serving Him is all that matters.

One of the most difficult things in my life was in regards to dating and relationships. All through high school and college I had many friends. I tended to seek out female friends more than male friends, and I suppose that I have had more than some people. However, I longed for the more intimate companionship of a lover. I had a few girlfriends, but none were serious except for Joni. You cannot know the amount of social pressure that exists (especially in churches) to get married in college, unless you have already felt that pressure. After I graduated from college, I really thought that my opportunity for finding a mate had passed. I had just about convinced myself of that when my feelings again stirred for my best friend, Joni. She graduated about a year after me and moved back home. We did everything together, and because of our amazing friendship, we grew to love each other in a way that I had never experienced before. Now, some will tell you that was "God's timing." As a side note, I believe people that say that God has a hand in every event of your life have not read Ecclesiastes 9:11, however, that debate is for another time. What I will say is that I have never prayed for anything in my life as much as I prayed for a Godly wife. I prayed for a Godly wife almost nightly, and these were not dry, passionless prayers. I would pray to the point of desperation in my more depressed times. I never truly believed that my prayer would be answered, but God is bigger than our doubts. I, now, have no doubt that Joni is the answer to those prayers.

I do not think it was low self-esteem that led me to my doubting, but rather, a misconception of love. Up until Joni, I had never understood real love. Not that I didn't have an incredible example in my parents...I did. It's that I did not see how a woman would ever want to be MY wife. I could not see what would be in it for her. The special things that she would have to do in this relationship would surely not be worth whatever it was that I had to offer. Ok, so maybe it was low self-esteem. I could not have been more wrong! I have a wife who loves me, takes care of me, and above all else, loves God. Quite often, I hear comments of how sweet and loving she is to me. I always reply, "I know, that's why I married her."

What is so amazing to me is that while she does do quite a bit of caretaking, that caretaking is not what the relationship is about. All of the things that had me worried are not even issues for her. At one point when we were dating we were talking about marriage. I asked her if she knew what all was involved in taking care of me. She replied, "I wouldn't have let this relationship begin if I hadn't already thought about and accepted that." I guess it looks a bit cold in print, but those words were among the warmest words I'd ever heard. Here is a woman who has already looked past my exterior and has chosen to love me for who I really am.

I can say that our few months as husband and wife have been bliss. We rarely argue, but when we do, it is usually amidst laughter! We say that is the best way to argue. When the air is tense, often one of us will do or say something that gets the other person to laugh. Once the laughter cuts the tension out, we are able to speak to each other without being in the defensive stance. Things get worked out quite a bit faster when you pull out the emotional tension in a situation.

I always thought that my physical needs would get in the way of a marriage relationship. As if she knew all my worries, Joni calms every one of them. Sure, we have had a few awkward moments, but Joni's grace and patience have made all of those moments seem like the easiest times of my life. I really never knew that a relationship like this could exist.

I write all this to say, "Never give up!" I mentioned earlier that there were many times when I was ready to throw in the towel in regards to finding love. I met, and dated, many an immature woman who could not see past my outward appearance. (I'm sure there are many immature men out there, too, but I can't speak from dating experience for them.) Not all of them were immature. Some relationships that I had never did "click." Others were corrupted by the circumstances of the time and place we found ourselves in. All of these failures, though, did not help my hope of ever finding the right person. I gave up, but in giving up, I found true love.

You see, in ceasing the seemingly endless search, I let down my guard and allowed my best friend in to know the real me. I was not pretending to be someone else as I had on many previous dates. We were just friends, and that made the stress of dating disappear. It was a year after doing almost everything together that we both decided this friendship had become much more. I had hopes that it would head the way it did, but never belief or faith that it would. My best friend is now my wife, and I couldn't be happier. Thank You, God.

Beyond dating and relationships, never give up on life. God will sustain you through good times and bad times. Hear me when I say this, I KNOW bad times. Most of my life had been wonderful, but there have been horribly cruel moments that have made me want to lash out at the world. I won't go into to detail because I prefer not to relive the past. Know this, God is MY strength. He gets me through each and every day, and I honestly do not know where I would be without Him. In Psalm 18:1-2, David writes,

> "I love you, O LORD, my strength.
> The LORD is my rock, my fortress and my deliverer;
> my God is my rock, in whom I take refuge.
> He is my shield and the horn of my salvation, my stronghold."

That is my God! He is my foundation and my strength. I would not be as happy as I am nor as confident as I am without Him. I thank my parents for passing this faith to me, my friends for always being there for me, my wife for her undying love, but MOST of all, I thank my God for always being there for me.

Again, I say, Thank You, God.

13

HANNAH –
GRACE INDEED

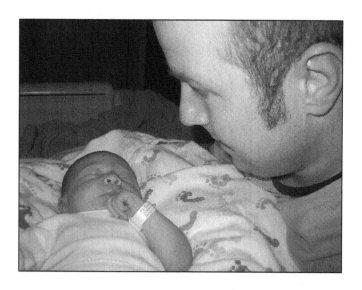

In the early summer of 2007, Chet and Joni told us that Joni was pregnant. They had started the process to adopt a child when they got the good news. Of course, they had to stop that process and concentrate on preparing for Hannah.

Hannah means "grace" or "favor," and they knew from the first that she was God's statement of favor toward them. The pregnancy was a delightful time. I have never seen a mother enjoy being pregnant more than Joni did.

On March 6, I got the call to come to Baylor Hospital and wait for the arrival of our eighth grandchild. Unfortunately, Hannah tried to enter the world with one arm coming out first. The doctor explained that could be a major problem with pressure on the umbilical cord. So, Joni quickly underwent caesarian surgery. Still, this was a wonderful. Soon, Chet, the Sneeds, and Judy and I watched through a nursery window while the nurses did their wonders on Hannah, and no father has ever been more excited than was Chet.

A Big Problem

Soon after Joni got home from the hospital, she began to be quite ill. A complication from the surgery had caused her to be filled with peritonitis. We rushed her back to the hospital, and she spent several days in Intensive Care. We prayed fervently, and the doctors found the right antibiotic. Soon, Joni was home again, and gained strength quickly. Two surgeries in one week were taxing on Joni, but she handled it all with grace and strength.

One day when Chet and Joni had gone back for a checkup with the surgeon, they over heard him say to his nurse that

Joni had been close to death. When Chet and I were alone, I asked him if he had realized while they were in the hospital how serious Joni's condition was. He quickly answered, "Of course." I said, "You were always so positive and bright through it all. You never appeared to be worried or fearful. How did you do it?" I am so proud of him for his answer. Chet said, "I refused to think about the possible negative results. My job was to lift her by my attitude. I chose to be happy and believe that we would get positive results." Then, I realized that while Judy and I had been truly scared, we never presented anything but a positive picture for Chet.

We all tried to figure ways for Chet to hold his baby, and get the benefit of "hands on" contact with her. We wanted him to be able to hold Hannah close to him. Eventually, he told us that he and Joni would figure that out. One day shortly after Hannah's birth, I walked into the hospital room and saw a beautiful sight. He and Joni were on her hospital bed. Chet had Hannah's head cradled between his  feet. She was facing him with her feet extending up on his stomach. He was leaning over toward her and talking to her. He was enjoying his daughter as much as any father could.

They have continued beautiful contact, and a great relationship is developing. Chet's skill with his feet allows him to feed Hannah, and lift her up in the air to play "Super Hannah."

When we travel to present Chet's story to audiences, we proudly display Hannah. Joni is amazing. She can take care of Hannah and get ready to sell books, CDs and DVDs at the same time. Of course, when the sales actually start, one of the grandparents tries to be close to care for Hannah while Chet and Joni talk to people who come to their display.

From a very early age, Hannah has seemed to be fascinated by her dad's singing. Chet was leading singing at the Plymouth Park Church of Christ when they had Hannah. In some of her early months, she would get still and quiet when she heard Chet's voice on the microphone. They used to tease the preacher because Hannah would get fussy when the preaching started. Now, at nine months, she still sits up and smiles while Chet is leading singing.

At first, Hannah would sleep while both Chet and Joni worked in their office. Then, in a few months, Hannah began to demand more attention as she stayed awake more. Now, she has started to crawl, and Chet and Joni will face a new, exciting world. Chet will tell you quickly that they look forward to each new day and each stage of development in this child, God's additional gift of goodness to the McDoniels.

Chet Says: Hannah is an amazing gift. I didn't really believe I was ready for children. I knew I wanted to have kids, but even with my postive, can-do attitude, I was concerned regarding how I would provide for a child in the same way her mother can. The first thing I learned was that no father can provide like a mother can. The bond that Joni and Hannah share is amazing, and I love watching them from across the room when they don't know I'm there.

Beyond that, I found that we would figure out how to handle each situation as it came. Joni encouraged me to try things out with Hannah to see what would work best, and both of them have been very patient as we three learn how to be a family. Hannah now crawls over and sits in my lap as we play. Nothing could warm my heart more, and I am so thankful for my beautiful daughter, my wonderful wife, and a loving God who shares every moment with us.

When Joni was in the hospital, I tried to do everything I could to show her my confidence that things would be okay. I picked up a technique for dealing with fear and it helped me tremendously while in the hospital. Another speaker once said that when you are in a dangerous situation, allow your body's natural fear to come in and take over your thoughts for five seconds. Close your eyes, and allow yourself to feel that fear. Count to five, open your eyes, and say to yourself that those five seconds will be the only time you are fearful during this situation. You felt the fear, you tasted it, and since it cannot help you, it is time to move on. I was able to show a positive, confident attitude to Joni because I believed everything was going to be okay. I also believed that my fear wouldn't help the situation one bit. If things hadn't turned out okay, I would have dealt with that later...but in the meantime, I had an important duty to my wife. I thank the Lord for the strength that he gave all of us, and for the outcome.

Joni and I now joke that when Hannah is acting up in the future, we'll have to tell her how much trouble she caused when she first arrived! ☺

14

TO GET THE MESSAGE OUT

When Chet was still a baby, a few friends tried to get me to "go on the road" with the story of his birth. I felt that they were way too early with their suggestion. Yet after we let years pass, I still found myself putting off speaking about Chet's life. Part of the reason for delaying was that Chet was still in the formative years. I kept saying that his story was too unfinished. When Chet was in high school, I started writing the first edition of this book. I experienced several delays, and I had trouble finding a publisher.

One of the delays was that Chet was not very interested. He never asked me not to write the story. When I mentioned his limb deficiencies from the pulpit, he approved of my using him. Yet, when I talked to him about going to churches and presenting his story, I found little or no interest. After he finished college and entered the work force, Chet began to see a need. He had already learned that he enjoyed leading worship. Primarily, leading worship in churches of Christ means leading singing, however, more and more Chet found the need to talk. Sometimes, he was presenting a transitional thought, and sometimes he was talking about a song he was going to lead. He soon found that he had a talent for communicating with audiences. Of course, his majoring in the field of radio, television, and film had prepared him for being before audiences.

When Chet consented to begin this ministry of helping others by telling his story, he was worshipping at the Richland Hills Church of Christ, a 5,000 member church. We asked if we could take a Wednesday night "Summit," have Chet lead the worship team, and tell his story, including some basic lessons that naturally flow from the story. The evening could not have gone better. The praise team at Richland Hills is one of the best, and they all knew Chet already. In fact, he had sung with them before, and had even led the group at one or two

special events. The singing was fantastic. Then, Chet and I
sat in straight chairs before the audience and told his story. I
told most of the first part since we began with the events of
his birth. We often joke, saying that Chet does not remember
his birth very well. As the story continued, Chet told more
and more of the events of his life and the attitudes he had
learned. Finally, I left the stage, and Chet finished the message by himself. Later, Chet got the DVD of the
presentation, took out any remarks that applied only to that
occasion, and we make the DVD of that presentation available on the website, www.allheneedsforheaven.com.

As we "debriefed" the evening, Chet announced that he had
found a calling. He said, "I was made to do what we did to-
night." Immediately, we started going to churches with the
story, using the same format. Soon, opportunities began to
present themselves in arenas other than churches. Chet has
presented his story to business groups and employee groups.
We have gone to schools and spoken to students. Then,
Chet decided to contact a speakers' bureau for more opportunities. He even resigned his work as the worship leader at
the Plymouth Park Church of Christ so that he would be
available to accept more invitations to travel and tell the
story.

At first, both of us had some difficulty thinking of the ministry as a business. We want to see it as ministry always. In I
Corinthians 9:7-12, Paul teaches that ministers should be paid
by those to whom they minister. Still, the thought of charg-

ing for telling the story seemed crass. Even today, we will speak at churches for whatever they want to pay as long as they give us the privilege of selling books, CDs, and DVDs. Chet has an agent that makes financial arrangements with businesses and other groups. We recognize that to be able to get the message out, we need to charge. Someday, Chet may need to spend all of his working time telling his story. Yet, we want to view these presentations as ministry. If this is not a ministry, neither of us would want to continue the effort. The reason for telling the story is to help others. It is a message that needs to be told, and the ministry, business side included, is developing nicely.

I marvel as I sit beside Chet on stage before an audience and listen to him tell them about life from his perspective. He has surprised me several times, even during our presentations. The title of the book comes from a statement I used several times trying to encourage Judy and myself. I used to say, "He does not have all he needs for life here, but he has all he needs for heaven." I have questioned the accuracy of that statement after listening to him tell about his life.

I am not blind to the obvious deficiencies of his body. He says, in talking to audiences, that he faces problems when he wants something that is on a high shelf. Recently, I had to leave my office and drive quickly to an office building three miles away to help him. Another driver had parked on the diagonal, solid, white stripes next to his van, thus blocking his access to the wheelchair lift. He needed me to back his van far enough for the lift to clear. The story not only illustrates Chet's need for help in some areas, but will serve a bigger purpose. When I arrived at the office building where Chet was waiting for me to back his van, he was smiling. The improperly parked car could not spoil Chet's day! Chet can pay someone to reach items on high shelves or call a family member to move his van, but he, alone, can determine to keep smiling and enjoying his life when someone blocks his access.

When I see his reactions in situations like that one or when I hear his message, I am reminded that Chet is not as handicapped as many able-bodied persons are. We need to learn from him, not just about heaven, but about how to live now. Sometimes, I think Chet has all he needs for heaven, and he has all he needs for this life, too.

7096274R0

Made in the USA
Charleston, SC
20 January 2011